책속 음원
바로 듣기!

음원 듣기 & 온라인 단어 학습

남다른 학습법으로
기적 같은 실력을 보장하는

기적의 영어리딩

체계적인 6단계 커리큘럼

	1 with 파닉스	2 with 주제 어휘	3 with 문장 패턴
목표	큰소리 리딩으로 문자 해독력을 높여요	리딩의 재미를 알며 기초 어휘력을 쌓아요	필수 문형을 접하며 문장 이해력을 높여요
리딩 소스	일상 이야기, 만화, 동화, 서사 논픽션 읽기	일상 이야기, 만화, 동화, 서사 논픽션 읽기	초대장, 포스터, 규칙 등의 정보·지식이 결합된 스토리 읽기
난이도	AR 0.5~1.0 Lexile BR~50 Words 50~70 (6p)	AR 0.7~1.5 Lexile 25~200 Words 70~90 (6p)	AR 1.3~2.3 Lexile 125~400 Words 90~110 (4p)
성취 수준	기초 어휘 180개	초등 3~4학년 교과서 수준 필수 어휘 180개	초등 5~6학년 교과서 수준 필수 어휘 200개

✓ 독해력 성장의 핵심 과정을 탄탄하게 밟아가는 6단계 리딩 프로그램

✓ 기적만의 3-Step 완전학습 시스템으로 확실한 학습 성과를 보장!

✓ 새 교육과정을 연계한 콘텐츠로 리딩 기초부터 중학 수준까지 저절로 완성!

✓ 적정 학습분량과 친절한 학습안내로 혼자서도 끝까지 완주 가능

4 with 문장 구조

다양한 글감을 읽으며 문장 구성력을 키워요
일상 소재의 실용문, 짧은 논픽션 읽기
AR 2.3~3.3 Lexile 420~620 Words 100~130
고학년 독해력 완성

5 with 문법

글을 논리적으로 이해하여 핵심을 파악해요
교과 연계된 최신 소재의 정보글 읽기
AR 3.0~3.9 Lexile 550~680 Words 130~150
예비중 리딩 · 문법 통합

6 with 서술형 영작

읽은 내용을 바탕으로 정리하는 표현력을 길러요
교과 연계된 최신 소재의 정보글, 의견글 읽기
AR 3.7~4.7 Lexile 650~780 Words 150~180
중학 독해 · 서술형 시험 대비

리딩 첫 시작부터 독해력 완성까지!

기본 다지기 — 영어와 친해지는 스토리 리딩으로 기본 바탕을 튼튼히!

Level 1 Level 2 Level 3

기적의 영어리딩 Level 1~3

- 초등 저학년의 영어 성장을 위한 리딩 기초 학습서
- 일상 이야기, 카툰, 동화 등 흥미로운 스토리로 리딩을 즐겁게 시작
- 따라가면 저절로 학습이 완성되는 3-STEP(읽기-이해-확장) 매일 학습
- 리딩의 기본기를 탄탄히 하는 파닉스 → 어휘 → 문장을 순차적으로 강화

실력 완성하기 — 논픽션 리딩으로 읽고 이해하고 표현하는 힘 기르기!

기적의 영어리딩 Level 4~6

- 초등 고학년의 문해력 완성과 중학 영어로의 연결을 돕는 리딩 심화 학습서
- 다양한 실용문과 정보글을 읽으며 글의 구조를 시각화하고 핵심을 파악하는 힘 강화
- 읽은 내용을 바탕으로 정리하고 표현하는 서술형 영작 훈련
- 문장 구조 → 논리적 이해 → 표현력 확장으로 이어지는 단계별 아웃풋 설계

3A

90~110 words
AR 1.3~2.3

기적의 영어리딩

with 문장 패턴

길벗스쿨

기적만의

3-Step 완전학습 시스템

읽고, 이해하고, 확장하는 3-Step 시스템으로 겉핥기가 아닌 진짜 실력을 키웁니다. 하나의 지문을 3단계에 걸쳐 깊이 있게 학습하면서 콘텐츠를 제대로 소화합니다. 동시에, 리딩의 기본 바탕이 되는 파닉스-어휘력-문장력을 차례로 강화합니다. 단순한 읽기를 넘어 문해력 성장을 위한 핵심 학습이 통합적으로 이루어지는 학습법입니다.

Step 1. 읽기

단어 익히기

지문을 이해하는 데 필수적인 키워드를 먼저 학습합니다.

스토리 리딩

생활 속 규칙과 사회·문화 지식을 담은 이야기를 반복해서 듣고 읽으며 단어와 표현을 쉽게 체화합니다.

Step 2. 이해

Step 3. 확장

내용 확인 문제

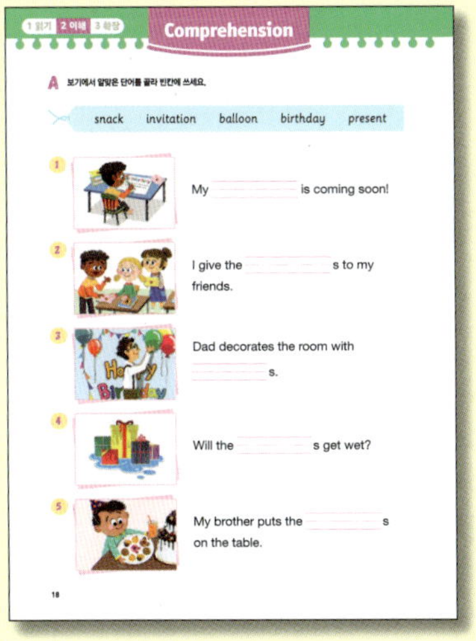

다양한 유형의 문제를 통해 읽은 내용을 충분히 이해하고, 단어 및 문장을 반복 학습하게 됩니다.

필수 문형 학습

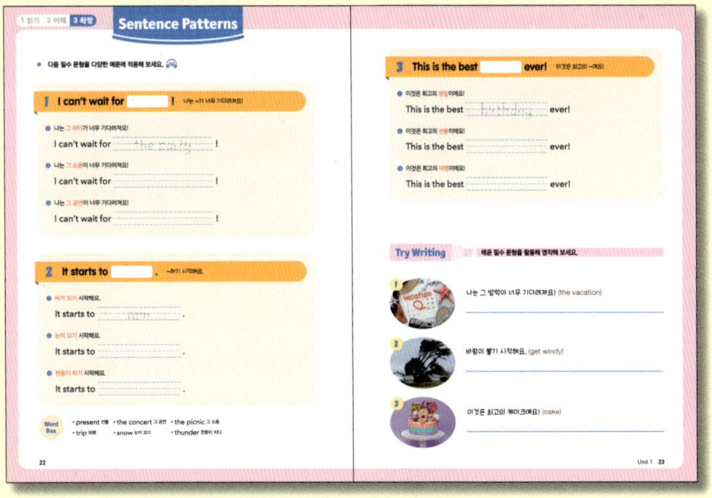

실력을 한 단계 더 끌어올리는 핵심학습을 짚고 갑니다.
Level 3에서는 문장 이해력을 높이는 필수 문형을 익히고 활용합니다.

Contents

Level 3A

How to Study

정보 · 지식이 담긴 흥미로운 스토리를 읽으며 문장 이해에 필수적인 다양한 문형을 익힙니다.

Level 3은 생활 속 규범, 사회 · 과학 지식이 결합된 이야기 지문으로 구성되어 있습니다. 흥미롭고 실용적인 이야기와 더불어 초대장 · 안내문 · 포스터 · 표 등 다양한 시각적 자료를 함께 접하며 읽고 이해하는 힘을 기릅니다.

또한 자주 쓰이는 교과서 필수 문형을 집중 학습합니다. 문형에 익숙해지면 리딩 속도와 이해력이 향상되고, 라이팅 활용 능력도 자연스럽게 길러집니다.

Step 1. 읽기
주요 단어를 익힌 다음 지문 따라 읽기

❶ **[Key Words]**에서 지문 이해에 중요한 단서가 되는 핵심 단어를 확인해요.

❷ **[온라인 단어 학습]**에서 단어를 반복 학습하며 뜻과 철자를 꼼꼼하게 익혀요.

❸ 간단한 문제를 풀며 단어를 잘 익혔는지 확인해요.

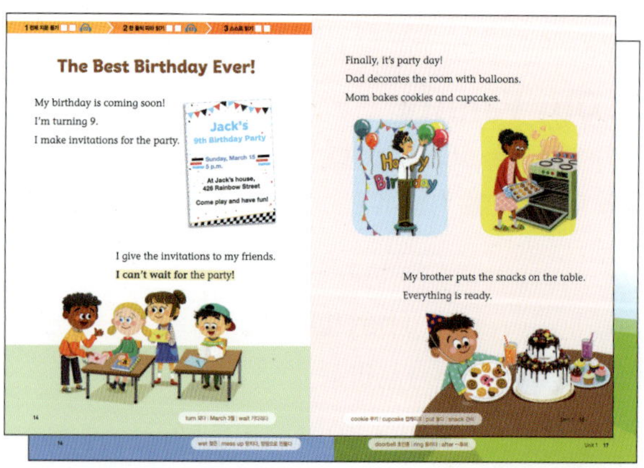

❹ 두 가지 버전의 음원을 잘 듣고 따라 읽어요.

- **[전체 지문 듣기]** 이야기를 잘 들으며 어떤 내용인지 파악해 보세요.
- **[한 줄씩 따라 읽기]** 한 문장씩 듣고 따라 읽어 보세요.
- **[스스로 읽기]** 처음부터 끝까지 정확하게 읽어 보세요.

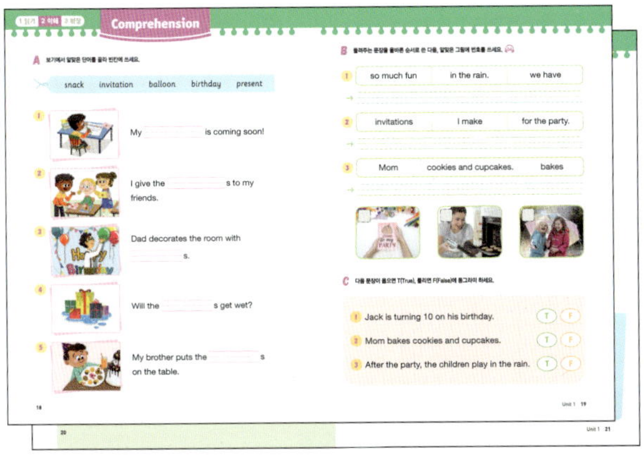

Step 2. 이해

문제를 풀며 지문을 제대로 이해하기

❶ [Comprehension]에서 여러 유형의 문제를 풀며 지문 이해도를 확인해요. 읽은 내용 정리하기, 반복 듣기, 생각 표현하기 코너를 통해 단어와 표현을 다지고 사고력도 함께 키워요.

❷ 문제 풀이 후 **[별책]** 정답지를 참고하여 채점하고 틀린 문제를 확인해 보세요.

Step 3. 확장

꼭 알아야 할 필수 문장패턴 익히기

❶ [Sentence Patterns]에서 필수 문형을 익히고 다양한 예문을 통해 연습해요.

❷ 배운 문형을 활용해 [Try Writing]에서 영작 연습을 해요.

❸ [Think More]에서 지문의 이야기 주제와 관련하여 한 발 더 나아간 액티비티를 풀며 다양한 정보와 지식을 탐구하고 관련 영어 표현을 익혀요.

[Review Test]

리뷰 테스트 2회분이 포함됩니다. Unit 1~4 테스트, Unit 5~8 테스트로 실력을 확인해 보세요.

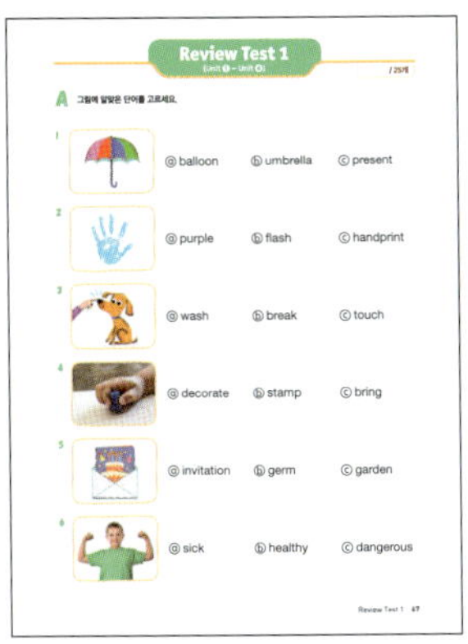

[별책: Practice Book]

스토리 속 문장을 의미 단위로 나누어 읽고 직접 써 보면서 문장 감각을 키우는 연습을 합니다.

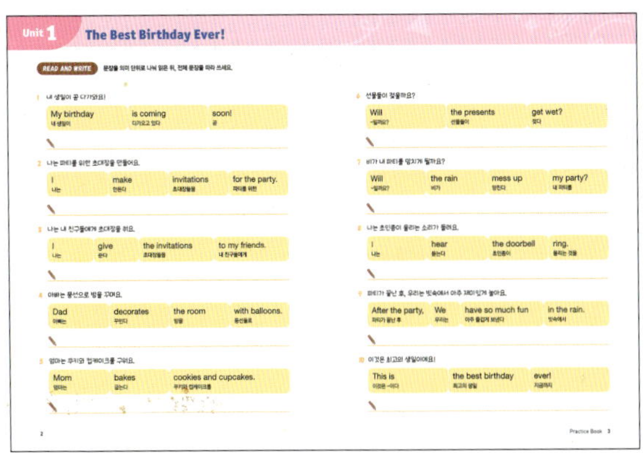

Study Plan

학습 완주를 위해 미리 학습계획을 세워 보세요.
26일 동안 집중하는 한 달 완성하기, 또는 주 3일 학습으로 차근차근 8주 완성하기!
나에게 맞는 방법을 정하고 진도표를 따라 끝까지 공부해 보세요.

26일 완성 학습 스케줄

Unit 1			Unit 2		
1. 읽기	2. 이해	3. 확장	1. 읽기	2. 이해	3. 확장
• 본책 p.12-17 • 온라인 단어 학습 월 일	• 본책 p.18-21 • 별책 p.2-3 월 일	• 본책 p.22-24 월 일	• 본책 p.26-31 • 온라인 단어 학습 월 일	• 본책 p.32-35 • 별책 p.4-5 월 일	• 본책 p.36-38 월 일
Unit 3			**Unit 4**		
1. 읽기	2. 이해	3. 확장	1. 읽기	2. 이해	3. 확장
• 본책 p.40-45 • 온라인 단어 학습 월 일	• 본책 p.46-49 • 별책 p.6-7 월 일	• 본책 p.50-52 월 일	• 본책 p.54-59 • 온라인 단어 학습 월 일	• 본책 p.60-63 • 별책 p.8-9 월 일	• 본책 p.64-66 월 일
Review Test 1 p.67-70					월 일
Unit 5			**Unit 6**		
1. 읽기	2. 이해	3. 확장	1. 읽기	2. 이해	3. 확장
• 본책 p.72-77 • 온라인 단어 학습 월 일	• 본책 p.78-81 • 별책 p.10-11 월 일	• 본책 p.82-84 월 일	• 본책 p.86-91 • 온라인 단어 학습 월 일	• 본책 p.92-95 • 별책 p.12-13 월 일	• 본책 p.96-98 월 일
Unit 7			**Unit 8**		
1. 읽기	2. 이해	3. 확장	1. 읽기	2. 이해	3. 확장
• 본책 p.100-105 • 온라인 단어 학습 월 일	• 본책 p.106-109 • 별책 p.14-15 월 일	• 본책 p.110-112 월 일	• 본책 p.114-119 • 온라인 단어 학습 월 일	• 본책 p.120-123 • 별책 p.16-17 월 일	• 본책 p.124-126 월 일
Review Test 2 p.127-130					월 일

8주 완성 학습 스케줄

Week	단계	학습 내용	날짜
Week 1 Unit 1	1. 읽기	• 본책 p.12–17 • 온라인 단어 학습	월 일
	2. 이해	• 본책 p.18–21 • 별책 p.2–3	월 일
	3. 확장	• 본책 p.22–24	월 일
Week 2 Unit 2	1. 읽기	• 본책 p.26–31 • 온라인 단어 학습	월 일
	2. 이해	• 본책 p.32–35 • 별책 p.4–5	월 일
	3. 확장	• 본책 p.36–38	월 일
Week 3 Unit 3	1. 읽기	• 본책 p.40–45 • 온라인 단어 학습	월 일
	2. 이해	• 본책 p.46–49 • 별책 p.6–7	월 일
	3. 확장	• 본책 p.50–52	월 일
Week 4 Unit 4	1. 읽기	• 본책 p.54–59 • 온라인 단어 학습	월 일
	2. 이해	• 본책 p.60–63 • 별책 p.8–9	월 일
	3. 확장	• 본책 p.64–66	월 일
	Review Test 1 p.67-70		월 일
Week 5 Unit 5	1. 읽기	• 본책 p.72–77 • 온라인 단어 학습	월 일
	2. 이해	• 본책 p.78–81 • 별책 p.10–11	월 일
	3. 확장	• 본책 p.82–84	월 일
Week 6 Unit 6	1. 읽기	• 본책 p.86–91 • 온라인 단어 학습	월 일
	2. 이해	• 본책 p.92–95 • 별책 p.12–13	월 일
	3. 확장	• 본책 p.96–98	월 일
Week 7 Unit 7	1. 읽기	• 본책 p.100–105 • 온라인 단어 학습	월 일
	2. 이해	• 본책 p.106–109 • 별책 p.14–15	월 일
	3. 확장	• 본책 p.110–112	월 일
Week 8 Unit 8	1. 읽기	• 본책 p.114–119 • 온라인 단어 학습	월 일
	2. 이해	• 본책 p.120–123 • 별책 p.16–17	월 일
	3. 확장	• 본책 p.124–126	월 일
	Review Test 2 p.127-130		월 일

Key Words를 확실하게 익히는 온라인 단어 학습!

온라인 학습으로 지문을 이해하는 데 필요한 단어들을 꼼꼼하게 익혀요. 단어의 철자와 의미를 정확하게 알게 돼요.

길벗스쿨 e클래스에서 오디오 바로 듣기

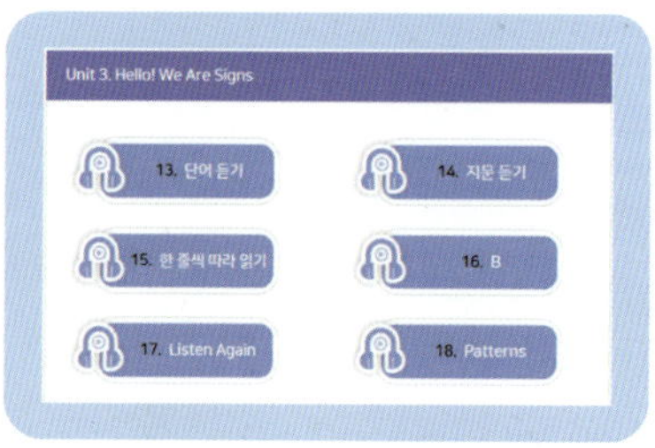

eclass.gilbut.co.kr에서 학습에 필요한 모든 음원을 제공합니다. 오디오 번호를 찾아 한 번만 탭 하면 해당 유닛의 단어와 스토리 음원을 바로 들을 수 있어요.

Practice Book으로 꼼꼼한 보충 학습!

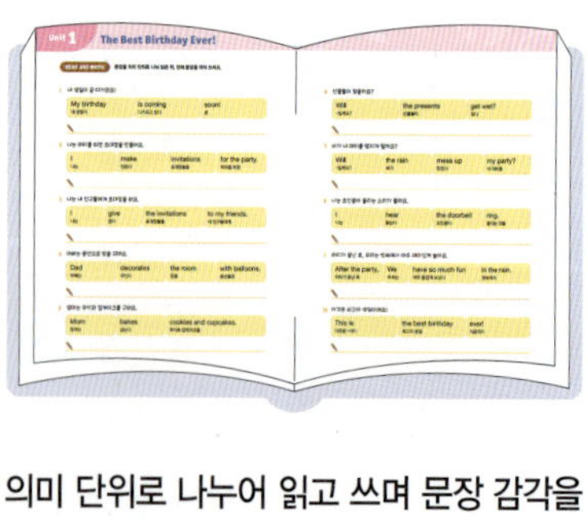

문장을 의미 단위로 나누어 읽고 쓰며 문장 감각을 키우는 별책 연습서를 제공해요.

Unit 1

The Best Birthday Ever!

STEP 1 읽기 핵심 단어를 익혀서 스토리 듣고 읽기

STEP 2 이해 읽은 내용을 점검하여 스토리 이해하기

STEP 3 확장 필수 문형 학습으로 문장 이해력 키우기

Key Words

- 다음 단어들을 하나씩 손으로 짚으며 잘 들어 보세요. 01

birthday

invitation

party

decorate

balloon

rain

present

umbrella

온라인 단어 학습

온라인 학습으로 단어를 꼼꼼히 익혀요.

A 단어와 우리말 뜻을 알맞게 연결하세요.

1	invitation	• •	파티
2	party	• •	초대장, 초대
3	present	• •	생일
4	birthday	• •	선물

B 다음 우리말 뜻에 맞는 단어를 찾아 동그라미 하고 한 번 쓰세요.

u	m	b	r	e	l	l	a
s	i	p	b	l	m	k	g
n	t	y	a	r	a	i	n
p	o	f	l	e	h	b	x
h	e	s	l	g	d	k	a
k	v	h	o	l	j	n	i
d	e	c	o	r	a	t	e
w	y	i	n	u	k	c	w

1 장식하다
d

2 풍선
b

3 비가 오다
r

4 우산
u

The Best Birthday Ever!

My birthday is coming soon!

I'm turning 9.

I make invitations for the party.

I give the invitations to my friends.

I can't wait for the party!

turn 되다 | March 3월 | wait 기다리다

Finally, it's party day!

Dad decorates the room with balloons.

Mom bakes cookies and cupcakes.

My brother puts the snacks on the table.

Everything is ready.

cookie 쿠키 | cupcake 컵케이크 | put 놓다 | snack 간식

Oh no! **It starts to** rain.

Will my friends come?

Will the presents get wet?

Will the rain mess up my party?

wet 젖은 | **mess up** 망치다, 엉망으로 만들다

Then, I hear the doorbell ring.

My friends are here with umbrellas and big smiles.

After the party, we have so much fun in the rain.

"**This is the best** birthday **ever!**"

doorbell 초인종 | ring 울리다 | after ~후에

Comprehension

A 보기에서 알맞은 단어를 골라 빈칸에 쓰세요.

> snack　　invitation　　balloon　　birthday　　present

1 

My ________ is coming soon!

2 

I give the ________s to my friends.

3 

Dad decorates the room with ________s.

4 

Will the ________s get wet?

5 

My brother puts the ________s on the table.

B 들려주는 문장을 올바른 순서로 쓴 다음, 알맞은 그림에 번호를 쓰세요. 04

1

so much fun	in the rain.	we have

→

2

invitations	I make	for the party.

→

3

Mom	cookies and cupcakes.	bakes

→

C 다음 문장이 옳으면 T(True), 틀리면 F(False)에 동그라미 하세요.

1 Jack is turning 10 on his birthday. T F

2 Mom bakes cookies and cupcakes. T F

3 After the party, the children play in the rain. T F

D 주인공의 기분이 어떻게 변했는지 보고, 알맞은 단어에 동그라미 하세요.

My birthday is coming soon! I'm (excited / sad).

It starts to rain.
I'm (happy / worried).

My friends are here.
I'm (surprised / sorry).

We have so much fun in the rain. We're (happy / tired).

• excited 신이 난 surprised 놀란 worried 걱정하는 tired 피곤한

Think & Say

생일에 내가 가장 좋아하는 활동은 무엇인가요?

- ☐ making a wish
- ☐ eating cake
- ☐ blowing out the candles
- ☐ having fun with friends

The best part of my birthday is ________________.

Listen Again

● 스토리를 다시 들으며 빈칸에 알맞은 단어를 써 넣으세요. 05

My ______ is coming soon! I'm turning 9. I make invitations for the ______.
I give the ______s to my friends. I can't wait for the party!

Finally, it's party day! Dad ______s the room with ______s. Mom bakes cookies and cupcakes.
My brother puts the ______s on the table.
Everything is ready.

Oh no! It starts to ______. Will my friends come?
Will the ______s get wet? Will the rain mess up my party?

Then, I hear the doorbell ring. My friends are here with ______s and big smiles.
After the party, we have so much ______ in the rain. "This is the best birthday ever!"

decorate
fun
invitation
party
birthday
snack
present
balloon
umbrella
rain

Sentence Patterns

● 다음 필수 문형을 다양한 예문에 적용해 보세요. 06

1 I can't wait for ______ ! 나는 ~가 너무 기다려져요!

① 나는 그 파티가 너무 기다려져요!

I can't wait for the party !

② 나는 그 소풍이 너무 기다려져요!

I can't wait for ______ !

③ 나는 그 공연이 너무 기다려져요!

I can't wait for ______ !

2 It starts to ______ . ~하기 시작해요.

① 비가 오기 시작해요.

It starts to rain .

② 눈이 오기 시작해요.

It starts to ______ .

③ 천둥이 치기 시작해요.

It starts to ______ .

Word Box

- present 선물
- the concert 그 공연
- the picnic 그 소풍
- trip 여행
- snow 눈이 오다
- thunder 천둥이 치다

3 This is the best ______ ever! 이것은 최고의 ~예요!

1. 이것은 최고의 생일이에요!
   This is the best birthday ever!

2. 이것은 최고의 선물이에요!
   This is the best ______ ever!

3. 이것은 최고의 여행이에요!
   This is the best ______ ever!

Try Writing

배운 필수 문형을 활용해 영작해 보세요.

1 

나는 그 방학이 너무 기다려져요! (the vacation)

______

2 

바람이 불기 시작해요. (get windy)

______

3 

이것은 최고의 케이크예요! (cake)

______

Think More

Chad's Birthday Invitation

★ 다음을 참고하여 생일파티 초대장을 완성하세요.

Whose birthday?

Chad

When?

July 8

3 o'clock

Where?

Chad's house

Come to
(   )'s Birthday Party!

Date: Saturday, (   ) (   )

Time: (   ) p.m.

Place: Chad's (   )
21 Rose Street, Garden Town

There will be cake, games, and fun!

Plus 생일파티 초대장에는 꼭 필요한 정보가 있어요. 바로 날짜, 시간, 장소예요. 날짜를 쓸 때는 요일-월-일-연도 순서로 써요. 시간은 오전이면 a.m.을, 오후면 p.m.을 써요. 파티가 열리는 장소도 잊지 말고 꼭 적어야 해요.

Unit 2

Leo Gets Sick

STEP 1 읽기 핵심 단어를 익혀서 스토리 듣고 읽기

STEP 2 이해 읽은 내용을 점검하여 스토리 이해하기

STEP 3 확장 필수 문형 학습으로 문장 이해력 키우기

Key Words

- 다음 단어들을 하나씩 손으로 짚으며 잘 들어 보세요. 07

dirt

wash

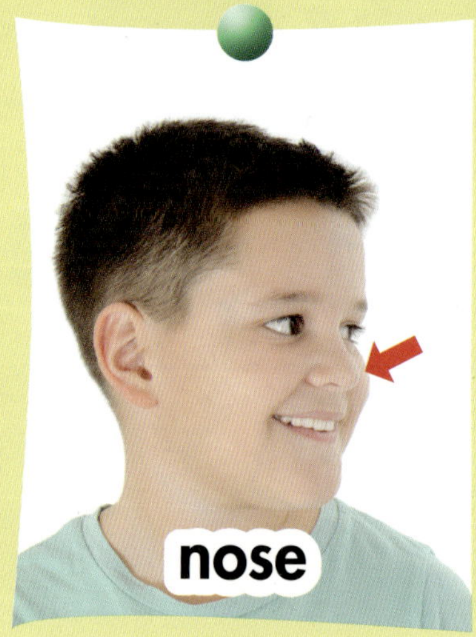
nose

sick

doctor

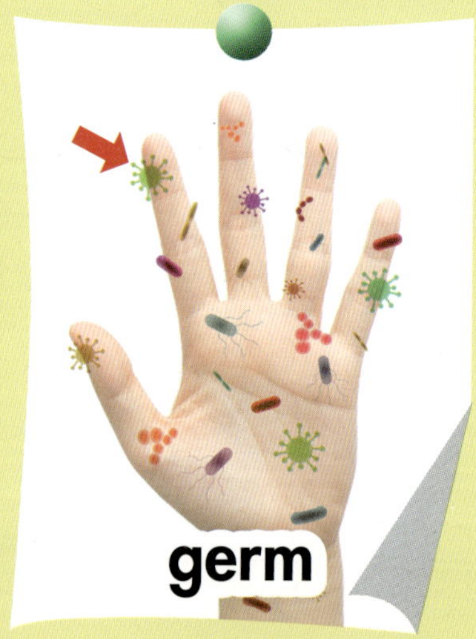
germ

healthy

soap

온라인 단어 학습

온라인 학습으로 단어를 꼼꼼히 익혀요.

A 단어와 우리말 뜻을 알맞게 연결하세요.

1	doctor	비누
2	healthy	세균
3	germ	건강한
4	soap	의사

B 우리말 뜻에 맞는 단어가 되도록 빈칸에 알맞은 글자를 쓰세요.

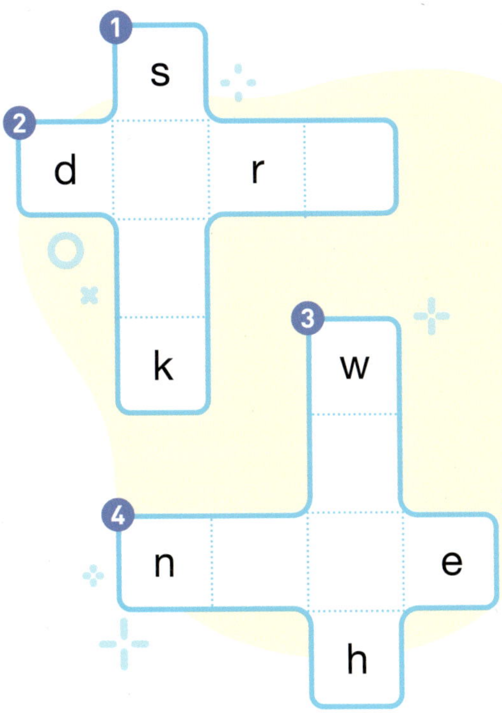

1 아픈

2 흙

3 씻다

4 코

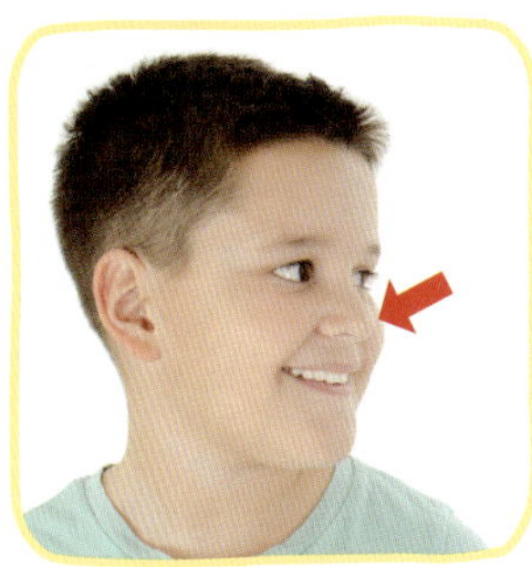

Leo Gets Sick

Leo loves playing outside.

He runs around the yard and digs in the dirt.

At lunch, Mom says, "Wash your hands!"

But Leo skips washing.

"I'll do it later," he says.

outside 밖에서 | yard 마당 | dig 파다 | skip 건너뛰다

Leo eats with his dirty hands.

Germs get on his sandwich and glass.

That afternoon, Leo's nose starts running.

His throat hurts.

"Why do I feel sick?" Leo wonders.

dirty 더러운 | get on ~에 묻다 | run 흐르다 | throat 목구멍 | wonder 궁금해하다

Mom takes Leo **to** the doctor.

The doctor says, "**Germs can make you** sick.

Please follow these healthy habits."

Wash your hands often

Drink lots of water

Eat healthy food

Get enough rest

Cover your mouth when you cough

follow 따르다 | habit 습관 | rest 휴식 | cover 덮다 | cough 기침하다

At home, Leo washes his hands with soap.

"This is easy!" he says.

Now, Leo follows the doctor's advice every day!

easy 쉬운 | advice 조언

Comprehension

A 보기에서 알맞은 단어를 골라 빈칸에 쓰세요.

dirty soap outside sick germ

1 

Leo loves playing ________.

2 

The doctor says, "________s can make you sick."

3 

"Why do I feel ________?" Leo wonders.

4 

Leo eats with his ________ hands.

5 

Leo washes his hands with ________.

B 들려주는 문장을 올바른 순서로 쓴 다음, 알맞은 그림에 번호를 쓰세요. (10)

1

starts	his nose	running.

→

2

takes him	to the doctor.	Mom

→

3

in the dirt.	he	digs

→

C 다음 문장이 옳으면 T(True), 틀리면 F(False)에 동그라미 하세요.

1 This story is about making a sandwich. T F

2 Leo washes his hands before eating lunch. T F

3 Leo says washing his hands is easy. T F

D 아래 문장들을 잘 읽고, 원인과 결과가 되도록 빈칸에 알맞은 기호를 쓰세요.

Cause(원인)		Effect(결과)
	→	Leo's nose starts running. His throat hurts.
Leo feels sick.	→	
The doctor gives him advice.	→	

ⓐ Mom takes Leo to the doctor.
ⓑ Leo eats with his dirty hands.
ⓒ Leo starts washing his hands every day.

Think & Say

이 글에서 가장 중요하게 배울 점은 무엇인가요?

- ☐ Go to your mom when you feel sick. (아플 때는 엄마에게 가세요.)
- ☐ Follow the doctor's advice. (의사의 조언을 따르세요.)
- ☐ Wash your hands to stay healthy. (건강하려면 손을 씻으세요.)

Listen Again

스토리를 다시 들으며 빈칸에 알맞은 단어를 써 넣으세요. 11

Leo loves playing ________. He runs around the yard and digs in the ________.
At lunch, Mom says, "________ your hands!"
But Leo skips washing. "I'll do it later," he says.

Leo eats with his dirty hands. Germs get on his sandwich and glass.
That afternoon, Leo's ________ starts running.
His throat hurts. "Why do I feel ________?"
Leo wonders.

Mom takes Leo to the ________. The doctor says, "________s can make you sick. Please follow these ________ habits."

At home, Leo washes his hands with ________.
"This is easy!" he says. Now, Leo ________s the doctor's advice every day!

wash
outside
sick
nose
germ
doctor
dirt
soap
healthy
follow

Sentence Patterns

● 다음 필수 문형을 다양한 예문에 적용해 보세요. 12

1 He loves ______-ing . 그는 ~하는 것을 매우 좋아해요.

❶ 그는 밖에서 노는 것을 매우 좋아해요.

He loves playing outside .

❷ 그는 자전거 타는 것을 매우 좋아해요.

He loves ______________ .

*마지막 글자가 자음+e로 끝나는 동사는 e를 빼고 -ing를 붙여요.

❸ 그는 아이스크림 먹는 것을 매우 좋아해요.

He loves ______________ .

2 Mom takes ______ to ______ . 엄마는 ~을 …에 데려가요.

❶ 엄마는 레오를 의사에게 데려가요.

Mom takes Leo to the doctor .

❷ 엄마는 나를 공원에 데려가요.

Mom takes ______ to ______ .

❸ 엄마는 내 남동생을 치과에 데려가요.

Mom takes ______ to ______ .

Word Box

- eat ice cream 아이스크림을 먹다
- my brother, the dentist 내 남동생, 치과
- ride his bike 자전거를 타다
- me, the park 나를, 공원
- sleepy 졸린
- tired 피곤한

3 They can make you ______. 그것들은 너를 ~하게 만들 수 있어.

① 그것들은 너를 아프게 만들 수 있어.

They can make you sick.

② 그것들은 너를 피곤하게 만들 수 있어.

They can make you ______.

③ 그것들은 너를 졸리게 만들 수 있어.

They can make you ______.

Try Writing

배운 필수 문형을 활용해 영작해 보세요.

1

그는 장난감 고치는 것을 매우 좋아해요. (fix toys)

______

2

엄마는 우리를 도서관에 데려가요. (us, the library)

______

3

그것들은 너를 슬프게 만들 수 있어. (sad)

______

Think More

Healthy Habits

★ 알맞은 말을 넣어 건강 습관을 완성해 보세요.

Wash your __________ often.

Wear a __________ on dusty days.

Drink plenty of __________.

Eat __________ food.

Get enough __________.

Cover your mouth when you cough.

water	mask	healthy	hands	rest

• dusty 먼지투성이의 plenty of 많은

Plus 건강을 지키려면 평소에 작은 습관이 중요해요. 손을 30초 이상 꼼꼼히 씻으면 세균의 90% 이상이 줄어든다고 해요. 또 물을 자주 마시면 코와 목을 촉촉하게 유지해 바이러스가 몸 속에 쉽게 들어오지 못한답니다. 이러한 건강 습관을 꾸준히 지키는 것이 튼튼한 몸을 만드는 첫걸음이에요.

Unit 3

Hello! We Are Signs

STEP 1 읽기 핵심 단어를 익혀서 스토리 듣고 읽기

STEP 2 이해 읽은 내용을 점검하여 스토리 이해하기

STEP 3 확장 필수 문형 학습으로 문장 이해력 키우기

Key Words

● 다음 단어들을 하나씩 손으로 짚으며 잘 들어 보세요. 13

sign

museum

touch

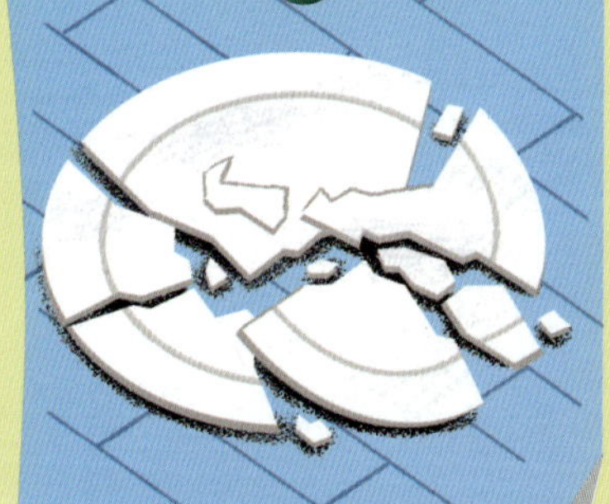

break

dangerous

bring

photo

flash

온라인 단어 학습

온라인 학습으로 단어를 꼼꼼히 익혀요.

A 단어와 우리말 뜻을 알맞게 연결하세요.

1	bring	•	• 반짝임
2	flash	•	• 위험한
3	dangerous	•	• 표지판
4	sign	•	• 가져오다

B 다음 우리말 뜻에 맞는 단어를 찾아 동그라미 하고 한 번 쓰세요.

p	h	o	t	o	y	r	h
w	k	s	j	f	a	d	e
l	u	b	n	v	e	k	p
c	f	r	t	o	u	c	h
m	q	e	g	l	f	s	b
b	i	a	t	j	c	z	i
s	n	k	q	v	y	o	n
m	u	s	e	u	m	p	w

1 박물관

m

2 만지다

t

3 사진

p

4 깨지다, 부서지다

b

Hello! We Are Signs

We are some "do not" signs in museums.

We have important messages.

Do you want to learn about us?

important 중요한 | message 메시지 | learn 알게 되다

I am the "No touching" sign.

I say, "**Don't touch** the things in the museum."

Some things can break easily.

I am the "No running" sign.

I say, "Walk, don't run."

Running inside can be dangerous.

easily 쉽게 | inside 안에서

I am the "No food" sign.

I say, "Don't bring or eat food inside."

Food can make a mess.

Look at me, the "No photos" sign.

I say, "Don't take photos."

Flash can damage art.

mess 엉망인 상태 | damage 손상을 주다 | art 미술품

We help keep museums safe.

Remember to follow the rules.

Thank you for listening to us.

keep 유지하다 | safe 안전한 | remember 기억하다

Comprehension

A 보기에서 알맞은 단어를 골라 빈칸에 쓰세요.

sign dangerous flash museum touch

1 

We are some “do not” __________s in museums.

2 

__________ can damage art.

3 

I say, “Don’t __________ the things in the museum.”

4 

We help keep __________s safe.

5 

Running inside can be __________.

B 들려주는 문장을 올바른 순서로 쓴 다음, 알맞은 그림에 번호를 쓰세요. 16

1

some things	easily.	can break

→

2

a mess.	food	can make

→

3

inside.	don't bring	or eat food

→

C 다음 문장이 옳으면 T(True), 틀리면 F(False)에 동그라미 하세요.

1. The "No running" sign tells you to walk inside. T F
2. The "No photos" sign tells you not to bring food. T F
3. The signs keep museums messy. T F

D 그림에 맞는 문장이 되도록 빈칸에 알맞은 단어를 찾아 쓰세요.

I say, "Don't ______________ the things in the museum."

I say, "Walk, don't ______________."

I say, "Don't take ______________s."

I say, "Don't ______________ or eat food inside."

photo　　run　　touch　　bring

Think & Say

주변에서 흔히 볼 수 있는 안내 표지판이에요. 각각 무엇을 의미할까요?

ⓐ Bicycle Lane (자전거 도로)

ⓑ Caution (주의)

ⓒ Exit (출구)

ⓓ Restroom (화장실)

Listen Again

● 스토리를 다시 들으며 빈칸에 알맞은 단어를 써 넣으세요. 17

We are some "do not" ______s in museums. We have important messages. Do you want to learn about us?

I am the "No touching" sign. I say, "Don't ______ the things in the museum." Some things can ______ easily.
I am the "No running" sign. I say, "Walk, don't ______." Running inside can be ______.

I am the "No food" sign. I say, "Don't ______ or eat food inside." Food can make a ______.
Look at me, the "No ______s" sign. I say, "Don't take photos." Flash can ______ art.

We help keep ______s safe. Remember to follow the rules. Thank you for listening to us.

run
damage
touch
break
museum
sign
bring
mess
photo
dangerous

Sentence Patterns

● 다음 필수 문형을 다양한 예문에 적용해 보세요. 18

1 Don't touch ______ . ~을 만지지 마세요.

① 미술품을 만지지 마세요.

Don't touch the art .

② 뜨거운 물을 만지지 마세요.

Don't touch ______ .

③ 칼을 만지지 마세요.

Don't touch ______ .

2 Remember to ______ . ~하는 것을 기억하세요.

① 규칙을 지키는 것을 기억하세요.

Remember to follow the rules .

② 네 숙제를 하는 것을 기억하세요.

Remember to ______ .

③ 네 책을 가져오는 것을 기억하세요.

Remember to ______ .

Word Box

- bring your book 네 책을 가져오다
- share 나눠주다
- the knife 칼
- do your homework 네 숙제를 하다
- come 오다
- the hot water 뜨거운 물

3 Thank you for ______ -ing . ~해줘서 감사합니다.

① 들어줘서 감사합니다.

Thank you for listening .

② 와줘서 감사합니다.

Thank you for ______ .

* 마지막 글자가 자음+e로 끝나는 동사는 e를 빼고 -ing를 붙여요.

③ 나눠줘서 감사합니다.

Thank you for ______ .

Try Writing

배운 필수 문형을 활용해 영작해 보세요.

1 네 점심을 먹는 것을 기억하세요. (eat your lunch)

______

2 벌레를 만지지 마세요. (the bug)

______

3 도와줘서 감사합니다. (help)

______

Museum Signs

★ 박물관에서는 어떤 규칙을 지켜야 할까요? 다음 상황에 알맞은 말을 완성하세요.

Please don't ________.

Sorry, you can't ________.

Please don't ________.

Please don't take ________ here.

eat　　run　　photos　　touch

Plus 박물관에서는 전시물을 보호하기 위해 사진 촬영이 제한되기도 해요. 카메라의 강한 불빛이 오래된 그림이나 유물을 손상시킬 수 있기 때문이에요. 또 사진을 찍는 동안 관람객의 길을 막거나 소음을 내어 방해가 될 수 있어요. 모두가 즐겁게 관람할 수 있게 하는 중요한 규칙이에요.

Unit 4

The Rainbow Garden

STEP 1 읽기 핵심 단어를 익혀서 스토리 듣고 읽기

STEP 2 이해 읽은 내용을 점검하여 스토리 이해하기

STEP 3 확장 필수 문형 학습으로 문장 이해력 키우기

Key Words

● 다음 단어들을 하나씩 손으로 짚으며 잘 들어 보세요. 19

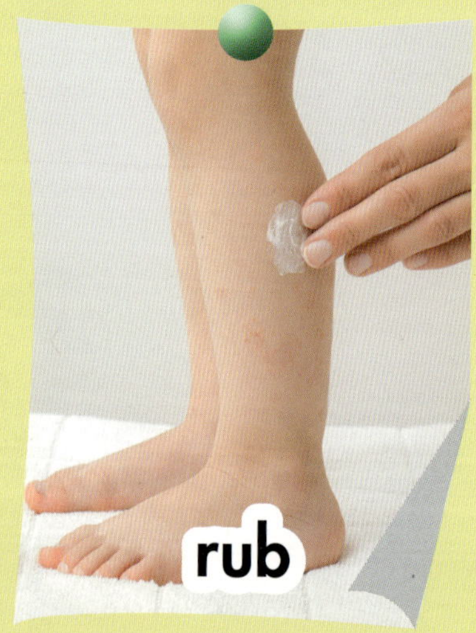

온라인 단어 학습

온라인 학습으로 단어를 꼼꼼히 익혀요.

A 단어와 우리말 뜻을 알맞게 연결하세요.

1 rainbow	손바닥 자국
2 rub	문지르다
3 paint	무지개
4 handprint	(물감 등을) 칠하다, 물감

B 우리말 뜻에 맞는 단어가 되도록 빈칸에 알맞은 글자를 쓰세요.

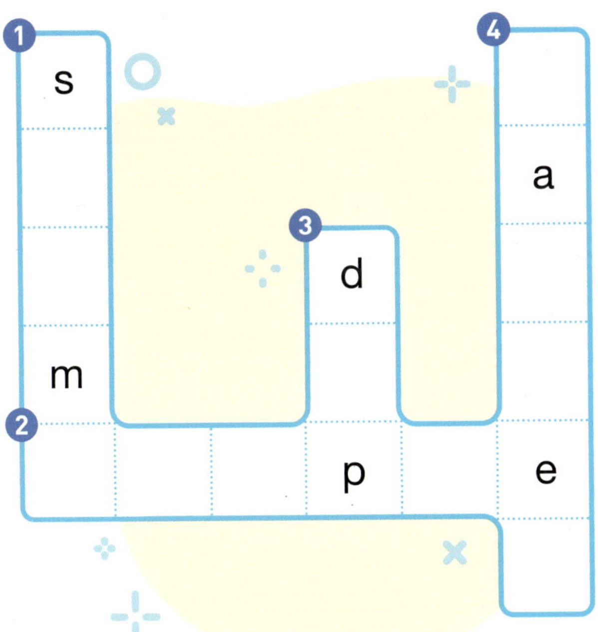

1 (도장 등을) 찍다

2 보라색의, 보라색

3 살짝 담그다

4 정원

The Rainbow Garden

Mia is painting a picture.

She loves yellow.

She paints her big paper yellow.

"It will be a beautiful yellow garden," she says.

paper 종이 | beautiful 아름다운

Her little sister, Luna, comes in.
Luna dips her hand in red paint.
She stamps it on the yellow picture.
Wow! The handprint turns orange!

turn 변하다

Luna uses her other hand.

She dips it in blue paint.

She stamps the picture again.

This time, **it turns** green!

Mia gets an idea.

She rubs both of Luna's hands together.

Now, the paint turns purple!

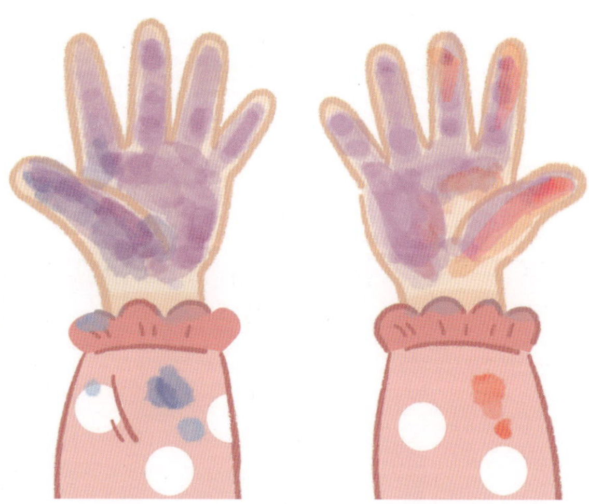

use 사용하다 | again 다시 | this time 이번에는 | idea 생각 | both 둘 다 | together 함께

"Luna, stamp your hands here!" Mia says.

Soon, the picture is done.

Look at the beautiful rainbow garden!

They smile and laugh together.

here 여기에 | soon 곧 | done 다 된 | laugh 웃다

Comprehension

A 보기에서 알맞은 단어를 골라 빈칸에 쓰세요.

rainbow rub stamp dip purple

1 

Luna ________s her hand in red paint.

2 

Look at the beautiful ________ garden!

3 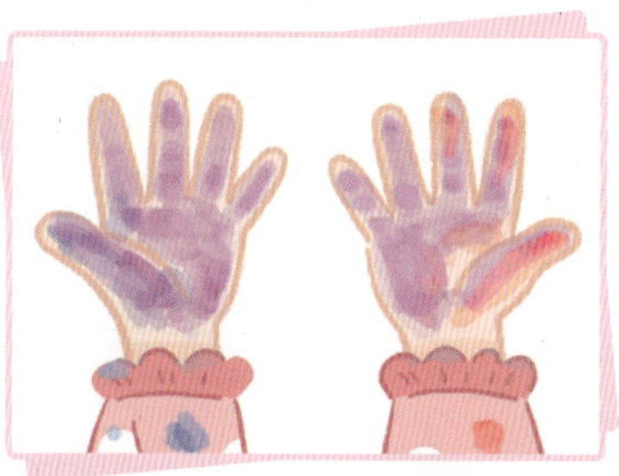

Now, the paint turns ________!

4 

Mia ________s both of Luna's hands together.

5 

Luna ________s the picture again.

B 들려주는 문장을 올바른 순서로 쓴 다음, 알맞은 그림에 번호를 쓰세요. 22

1

a beautiful	yellow garden.	it will be

→

2

yellow.	her big paper	she paints

→

3

orange!	the handprint	turns

→

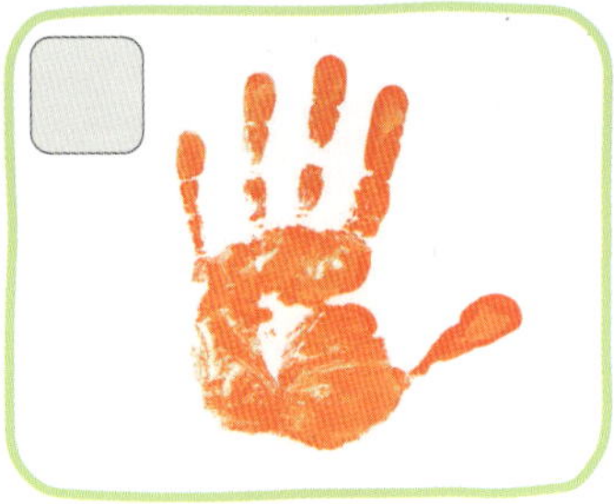

C 다음 문장이 옳으면 T(True), 틀리면 F(False)에 동그라미 하세요.

1 This story is about painting a colorful garden. T F

2 Mia paints her paper yellow. T F

3 Blue and yellow make green. T F

D 문장을 읽고, 그 결과로 나타난 색을 고르세요.

Actions (행동)	Colors (색깔)
Mia paints her paper yellow.	
Luna stamps red paint on the yellow picture.	
Luna stamps blue paint on the yellow picture.	
Mia rubs Luna's hands together. (red + blue)	

Think & Say

가장 좋아하는 색을 고르고, 그 이유를 말해 보세요.

- ☐ blue
- ☐ green
- ☐ red
- ☐ yellow
- ☐ purple
- ☐ ____________

I like ____________

because ____________.

Listen Again

● 스토리를 다시 들으며 빈칸에 알맞은 단어를 써 넣으세요. 23

Mia is painting a picture. She loves yellow. She ______s her big paper yellow.
"It will be a beautiful yellow ______," she says.

Her little sister, Luna, comes in. Luna ______s her hand in red paint. She ______s it on the yellow picture. Wow! The ______ turns orange!

Luna uses her other hand. She dips it in ______ paint. She stamps the picture again. This time, it turns ______!
Mia gets an idea. She ______s both of Luna's hands together. Now, the paint turns ______!

"Luna, stamp your hands here!" Mia says.
Soon, the picture is done. Look at the beautiful ______ garden! They smile and laugh together.

blue
purple
rainbow
rub
green
handprint
stamp
garden
paint
dip

Sentence Patterns

● 다음 필수 문형을 다양한 예문에 적용해 보세요. 24

1 She paints ______ ______. 그녀는 ~을 …으로 칠해요.

❶ 그녀는 큰 종이를 노랗게 칠해요.

She paints her big paper yellow.

❷ 그녀는 그 벽을 파랗게 칠해요.

She paints ______ ______.

❸ 그녀는 그 문을 초록색으로 칠해요.

She paints ______ ______.

2 It turns ______. 그것이 ~으로 변해요.

❶ 그것이 초록색으로 변해요.

It turns green.

❷ 그것이 주황색으로 변해요.

It turns ______.

❸ 그것이 보라색으로 변해요.

It turns ______.

Word Box

- the house 집
- the sky 하늘
- orange 주황색의
- purple 보라색의
- the wall, blue 그 벽, 파란
- the door, green 그 문, 초록색의

3 Look at ______ ! ~을 봐요!

❶ 저 정원을 봐요!

Look at the garden !

❷ 저 집을 봐요!

Look at ______ !

❸ 저 하늘을 봐요!

Look at ______ !

Try Writing

배운 필수 문형을 활용해 영작해 보세요.

1

그녀는 그 집을 빨갛게 칠해요. (the house, red)

______

2

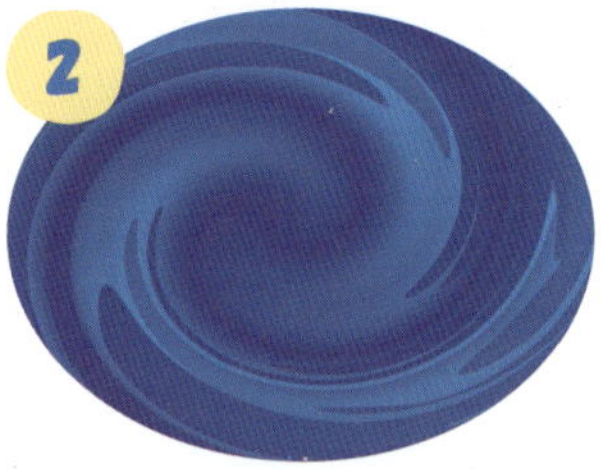

그것이 파랗게 변해요. (blue)

______

3

저 무지개를 봐요! (the rainbow)

______

Think More

Mixing Colors

★ 두 가지 색을 섞으면 어떤 색이 나올까요? 빈칸을 채워 보세요.

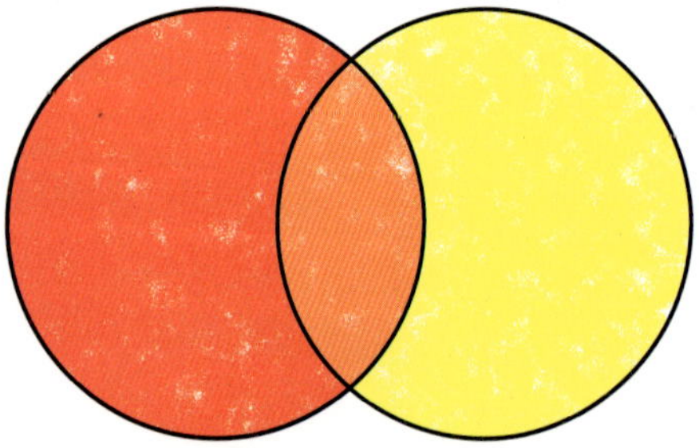

Mix red and yellow to make

______________.

Mix yellow and ______________

to make green.

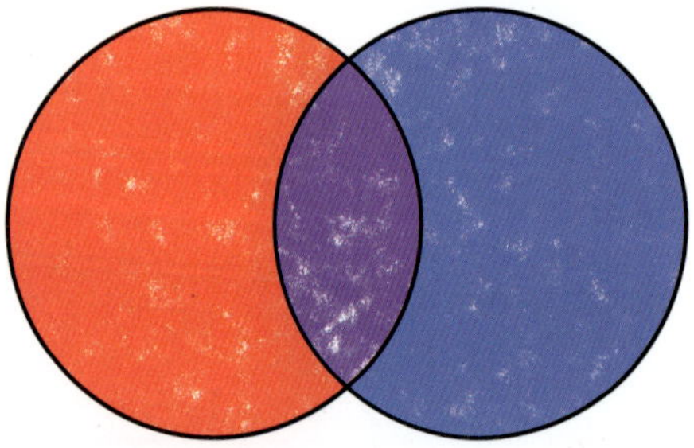

Mix ______________ and blue

to make ______________.

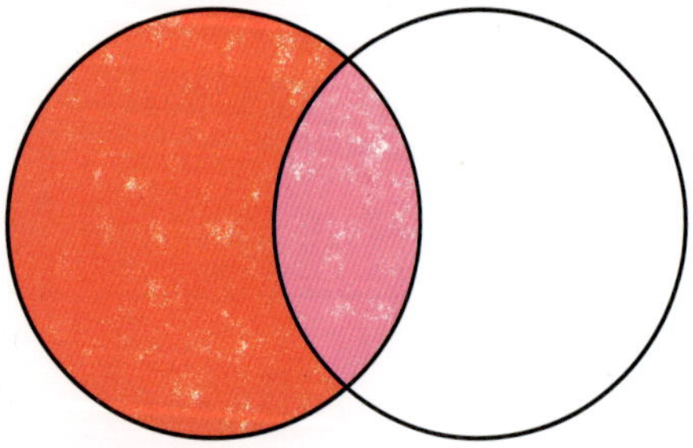

Mix red and white to make

______________.

Plus 빨강, 파랑, 노랑은 '삼원색'이라고 불러요. 삼원색은 다른 색을 섞어서 만들 수 없는 가장 기본이 되는 색이에요. 이 세 가지 색을 서로 섞으면 초록, 주황, 보라 등의 여러 가지 색을 만들 수 있어요. 그런데 세 가지 색을 모두 한꺼번에 섞으면 색이 점점 어두워져서 검은색이 돼요. 이것도 꼭 기억해야 할 색의 비밀이에요.

Review Test 1
(Unit ❶ – Unit ❹)

/ 25개

A 그림에 알맞은 단어를 고르세요.

1 

ⓐ balloon ⓑ umbrella ⓒ present

2 

ⓐ purple ⓑ flash ⓒ handprint

3 

ⓐ wash ⓑ break ⓒ touch

4 

ⓐ decorate ⓑ stamp ⓒ bring

5 

ⓐ invitation ⓑ germ ⓒ garden

6 

ⓐ sick ⓑ healthy ⓒ dangerous

B 그림을 보고 알맞은 문장을 고르세요.

1 

ⓐ I make invitations for the party.

ⓑ I give the invitations to my friends.

2 

ⓐ Mom brings him a sandwich.

ⓑ Mom takes Leo to the doctor.

3 

ⓐ "Don't touch the things in the museum."

ⓑ "Don't bring or eat food inside."

4 

ⓐ Luna paints the paper blue.

ⓑ Luna stamps her hand on the picture.

★★

C 알맞은 단어를 골라 문장을 완성하세요.

1 Leo washes his hands (ⓐ with ⓑ on) soap.

2 Mia is (ⓐ paint ⓑ painting) a picture.

3 Thank you for (ⓐ listen ⓑ listening) to us.

4 Oh no! It starts (ⓐ rain ⓑ to rain).

D 짧은 글을 읽고 질문에 알맞은 대답을 고르세요.

1 다음 글에서 I가 가리키는 표지판을 고르세요.

I am a sign in the museum.
I say, "Walk, don't run."
Running inside can be dangerous.

ⓐ

ⓑ

2 빈칸에 들어갈 알맞은 단어를 고르세요.

Luna dips her hand in blue paint.
She stamps it on the yellow picture.
It turns __________.

ⓐ green

ⓑ orange

3 빈칸에 들어갈 알맞은 단어를 고르세요.

The doctor says, "Germs can make you __________. Please follow these healthy habits."

ⓐ sick ⓑ tall

4 빈칸에 들어갈 알맞은 문장을 고르세요.

My birthday is coming soon! I make invitations for the party. I give the invitations to my friends. __________
____

ⓐ I can't wait for the vacation!

ⓑ I can't wait for the party!

E 필수 패턴을 활용해 우리말에 알맞은 영어 문장을 완성하세요.

Don't touch ______.	He loves ______.
It starts to ______.	Look at ______!

1 그는 밖에서 노는 것을 매우 좋아해요.

→ ______________________ playing outside.

2 미술품을 만지지 마세요.

→ ______________________ the art.

3 비가 오기 시작해요.

→ ______________________ rain.

4 저 정원을 봐요!

→ ______________________ the garden!

F 우리말에 알맞은 영어 문장을 쓰세요.

1 들어줘서 감사합니다. (for, you, thank, listening)

→ ______________________________________.

2 이것은 최고의 생일이에요! (the best, this, is, ever, birthday)

→ ______________________________________!

3 세균들이 너를 아프게 만들 수 있어. (can, germs, make, sick, you)

→ ______________________________________.

Unit 5

Spooky Halloween Toast

STEP 1 읽기 핵심 단어를 익혀서 스토리 듣고 읽기

STEP 2 이해 읽은 내용을 점검하여 스토리 이해하기

STEP 3 확장 필수 문형 학습으로 문장 이해력 키우기

Key Words

● 다음 단어들을 하나씩 손으로 짚으며 잘 들어 보세요. 25

toast

spread

add

mouth

ghost

raisin

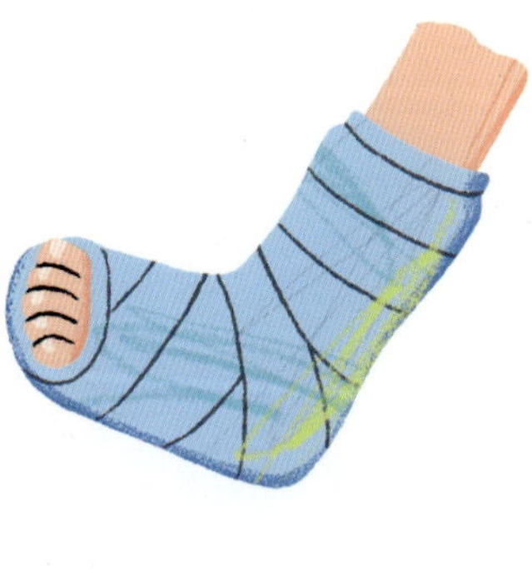
bandage

spooky

온라인 단어 학습

온라인 학습으로 단어를 꼼꼼히 익혀요.

A 단어와 우리말 뜻을 알맞게 연결하세요.

1 mouth		유령, 귀신
2 ghost		넣다, 추가하다
3 add		입
4 spooky		으스스한

B 다음 우리말 뜻에 맞는 단어를 찾아 동그라미 하고 한 번 쓰세요.

r	a	i	s	i	n	b	t
d	u	j	o	g	e	n	o
m	h	c	q	k	s	j	a
i	r	y	l	t	p	u	s
t	x	h	v	z	r	d	t
p	j	s	e	y	e	m	f
y	b	a	n	d	a	g	e
f	w	l	r	k	d	i	c

1 붕대

b

2 (버터 등을) 바르다

s

3 건포도

r

4 토스트

t

Spooky Halloween Toast

Let's make Halloween toast!

We're going to make fun monster faces.

These are easy and fun to make.

Are you ready?

monster 괴물 | face 얼굴

Avocado Monster Toast

First, spread avocado on a slice of toast.

Next, add olives for the eyes.

Finally, use bell pepper for the mouth.

Banana Ghost Toast

First, spread peanut butter on a slice of toast.

Next, cut a banana in half.

Put the halves on the toast.

Then, add raisins for the eyes.

slice 조각 | **half** 절반 (**halves** 반쪽들)

White Ghost Toast

First, spread cream cheese on a slice of toast.

Next, make a fun face with olives.

Now **it looks like** a ghost!

Mummy Toast

First, place ham on a slice of toast.

Next, add cheese strips like bandages.

Then, finish it with olives.

place 놓다 | strip 가느다란 조각 | finish 끝내다

All the spooky toast is ready!

Share the toast with your family and friends.

Have a spooky Halloween!

share 나누다

Comprehension

A 보기에서 알맞은 단어를 골라 빈칸에 쓰세요.

place ghost spread toast mouth

1 

First, __________ ham on a slice of toast.

2 

All the spooky __________ is ready!

3 

Now it looks like a __________ !

4 

Finally, use bell pepper for the __________ .

5 

First, __________ cream cheese on a slice of toast.

B 들려주는 문장을 올바른 순서로 쓴 다음, 알맞은 그림에 번호를 쓰세요. 28

1

like bandages.	add	cheese strips

→

2

spread	on a slice of toast.	peanut butter

→

3

raisins	for the eyes.	add

→

C 다음 문장이 옳으면 T(True), 틀리면 F(False)에 동그라미 하세요.

1 This story is about making Halloween toast. T F

2 Use ham for the monster's mouth. T F

3 Add cheese strips for the mummy's bandages. T F

D 설명을 잘 읽고 알맞은 토스트 이름을 빈칸에 쓰세요.

Avocado Monster Toast

Banana Ghost Toast

White Ghost Toast

Mummy Toast

Add cheese strips like bandages, and finish it with olives. [ ]

Spread avocado on a slice of toast, and add olives for the eyes. [ ]

Spread cream cheese on a slice of toast, and make a fun face with olives. [ ]

Think & Say

어떤 토스트를 만들고 싶나요? 토스트에 넣을 재료를 골라 보세요.

- [ ] banana
- [ ] raisins
- [ ] avocado
- [ ] olives
- [ ] mango
- [ ] cream cheese
- [ ] cheese
- [ ] ____________

My spooky toast will be delicious because it has ____________.

Listen Again

- 스토리를 다시 들으며 빈칸에 알맞은 단어를 써 넣으세요. 29

Let's make Halloween ________! We're going to make fun monster faces. These are easy and fun to make. Are you ready?

[Avocado Monster Toast] First, ________ avocado on a slice of toast. Next, add olives for the eyes. Finally, use bell pepper for the ________.

[Banana Ghost Toast] First, spread peanut butter on a slice of toast. Next, cut a banana in half. Put the halves on the toast. Then, add ________s for the eyes.

[White Ghost Toast] First, spread cream cheese on a slice of toast. Next, make a fun ________ with olives. Now it looks like a ________!

[Mummy Toast] First, place ham on a slice of toast. Next, ________ cheese strips like ________s. Then, finish it with olives.

All the ________ toast is ready! ________ the toast with your family and friends. Have a spooky Halloween!

face
add
spooky
raisin
mouth
ghost
spread
toast
share
bandage

Sentence Patterns

● 다음 필수 문형을 다양한 예문에 적용해 보세요. 30

1 Let's make ______ ! ~을 만들자!

① 핼러윈 토스트를 만들자!

Let's make Halloween toast !

② 샌드위치를 만들자!

Let's make ______ !

③ 피자를 만들자!

Let's make ______ !

2 We're going to ______ . 우리는 ~할 거예요.

① 우리는 재미있는 괴물 얼굴을 만들 거예요.

We're going to make fun monster faces .

② 우리는 컴퓨터를 사용할 거예요.

We're going to ______ .

③ 우리는 달걀을 살 거예요.

We're going to ______ .

Word Box

- a dragon 용
- a sandwich 샌드위치
- buy some eggs 달걀을 사다
- use the computer 컴퓨터를 사용하다
- a pizza 피자
- a cat 고양이

3 It looks like ______. 그것은 ~처럼 보여요.

❶ 그것은 유령처럼 보여요.

It looks like a ghost.

❷ 그것은 고양이처럼 보여요.

It looks like ______.

❸ 그것은 용처럼 보여요.

It looks like ______.

Try Writing

배운 필수 문형을 활용해 영작해 보세요.

1

쿠키를 만들자! (cookies)

______

2

그것은 호박처럼 보여요. (a pumpkin)

______

3

우리는 피아노를 연주할 거예요. (play the piano)

______

Think More

Let's Make Spooky Toast!

★ 요리 재료가 적힌 메모를 보고 완성된 토스트를 찾아 연결하세요.

- ☐ mashed avocado
- ☐ sliced bell pepper
- ☐ sliced olives

- ☐ blueberries
- ☐ raspberries
- ☐ sliced cucumber

- ☐ peanut butter
- ☐ sliced banana
- ☐ some raisins

- ☐ eggs
- ☐ sliced cucumber
- ☐ sliced ham

• mashed 으깬 blueberry 블루베리 raspberry 산딸기 cucumber 오이

Plus 핼러윈(Halloween)은 10월 31일로, 원래는 나쁜 귀신을 쫓기 위한 유럽의 전통에서 시작되었지만 지금은 즐거운 축제가 되었어요. 아이들이 괴물이나 유령처럼 분장을 하고 이웃집을 돌며 "Trick or treat!"라고 외치면 이웃들이 사탕을 나누어 준답니다.

Unit 6

A Trip to Grandma's House

STEP 1 읽기 핵심 단어를 익혀서 스토리 듣고 읽기

STEP 2 이해 읽은 내용을 점검하여 스토리 이해하기

STEP 3 확장 필수 문형 학습으로 문장 이해력 키우기

Key Words

- 다음 단어들을 하나씩 손으로 짚으며 잘 들어 보세요. 31

map

fence

park

right

corner

across

wave

waving 흔들고 있는

afraid

온라인 단어 학습

온라인 학습으로 단어를 꼼꼼히 익혀요.

A 단어와 우리말 뜻을 알맞게 연결하세요.

1	across	울타리
2	right	(손을) 흔들다
3	fence	건너서
4	wave	오른쪽으로, 오른쪽의

B 우리말 뜻에 맞는 단어가 되도록 빈칸에 알맞은 글자를 쓰세요.

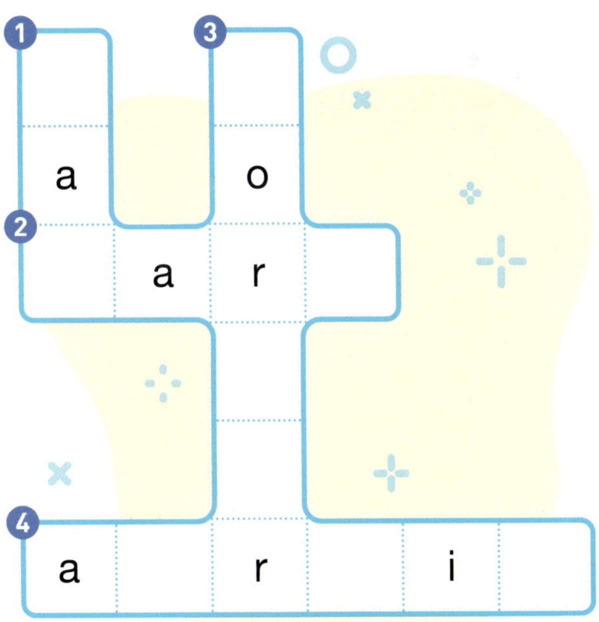

1 지도

2 공원

3 모퉁이

4 두려워하는

A Trip to Grandma's House

I'm going to Grandma's house on my own.

This map will help me find the way.

I live here, next to the house with a red fence.

Grandma's house is near the big park.

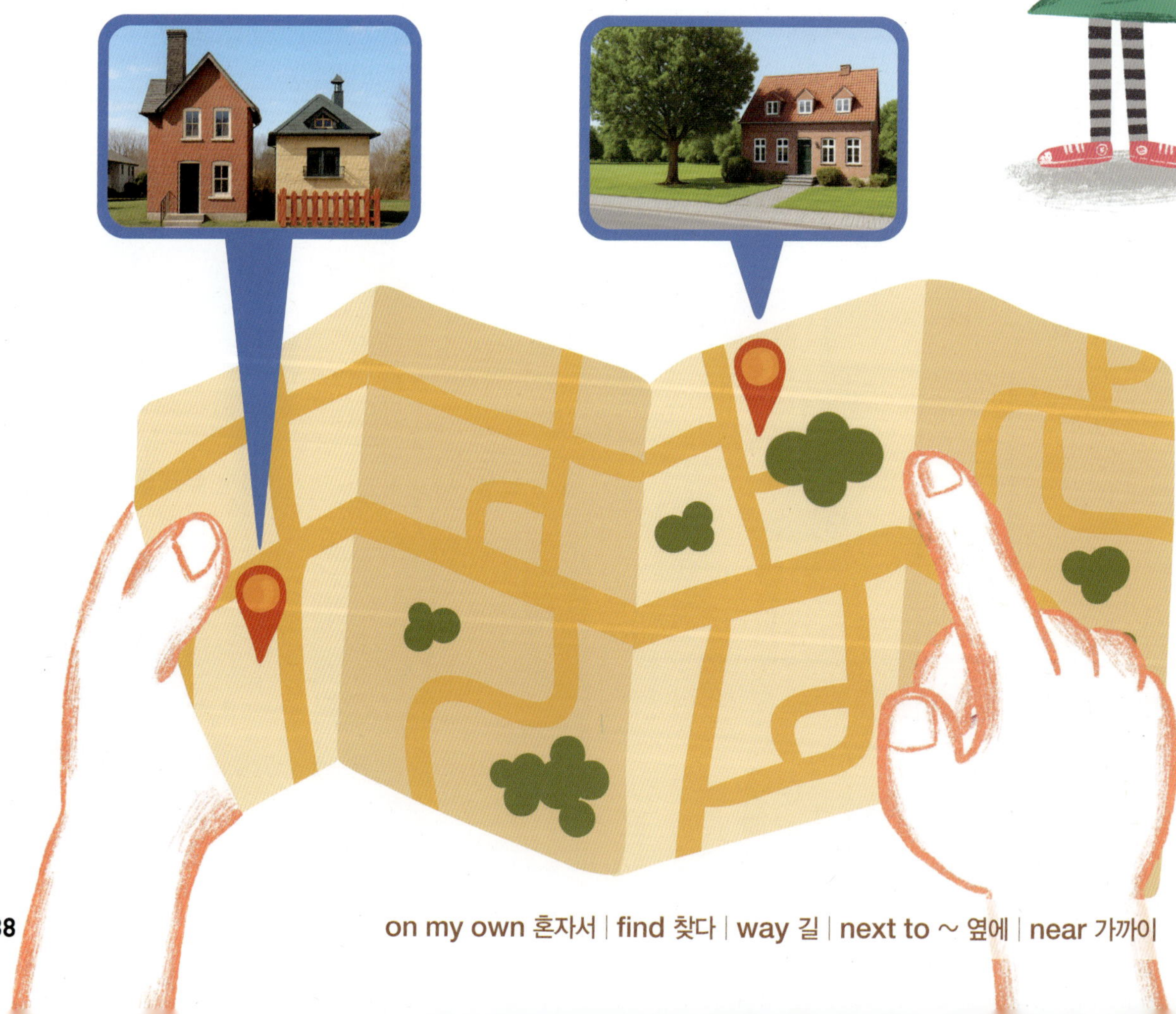

on my own 혼자서 | find 찾다 | way 길 | next to ~ 옆에 | near 가까이

First, I walk along Oak Street.

Then, I turn right onto Main Street.

Look! **There is** a bakery **on the corner.**

I turn left and walk toward the library.

turn 돌아서다 | bakery 빵집 | left 왼쪽으로, 왼쪽의 | toward ~쪽으로 | library 도서관

Grandma's house is across the street.

There is a big tree next to it.

Her house has a green door.

I see Grandma waving from her window.

At first, **I was afraid to** go alone.

But this map really helped me.

I can't wait to visit Grandma again!

Comprehension

A 보기에서 알맞은 단어를 골라 빈칸에 쓰세요.

across   map   corner   park   fence

1 

I live here, next to the house with a red __________.

2 

Grandma's house is __________ the street.

3 

This __________ will help me find the way.

4 

There is a bakery on the __________.

5 

Grandma's house is near the big __________.

B 들려주는 문장을 올바른 순서로 쓴 다음, 알맞은 그림에 번호를 쓰세요. 34

1

afraid	I was	to go alone.

→

2

next to	there is a big tree	Grandma's house.

→

3

Grandma waving	from her window.	I see

→

C 다음 문장이 옳으면 T(True), 틀리면 F(False)에 동그라미 하세요.

1 She uses a map to go to Grandma's house. T F

2 Grandma's house is near the big park. T F

3 Grandma's house has a red door. T F

D 지도를 보고, 할머니 집에 가는 방법을 순서대로 적으세요.

1 [ ] → 2 [ ] → 3 [ ] → 4 [ ]

ⓐ Turn right onto Main Street.
ⓑ Walk along Oak Street.
ⓒ Turn left and walk toward the library.
ⓓ Grandma's house is across the street.

Think & Say

혼자서 해 보고 싶은 일을 골라 문장을 완성해 보세요.

- [ ] take the bus
- [ ] walk my dog
- [ ] buy a snack at a store
- [ ] visit my friend

I want to ______________ by myself.

Listen Again

- 스토리를 다시 들으며 빈칸에 알맞은 단어를 써 넣으세요. 35

I'm going to Grandma's house on my own. This map will help me find the way. I live here, ________ to the house with a red ________. Grandma's house is near the big ________.

First, I walk along Oak Street. Then, I turn ________ onto Main Street. Look! There is a bakery on the ________. I turn left and walk toward the ________.

Grandma's house is ________ the street. There is a big tree next to it. Her house has a green door. I see Grandma waving from her ________.

At first, I was ________ to go alone. But this ________ really helped me. I can't wait to visit Grandma again!

right
next
park
fence
library
map
corner
across
afraid
window

Sentence Patterns

● 다음 필수 문형을 다양한 예문에 적용해 보세요. 36

1 There is ______ on the corner. 모퉁이에 ~이 있어요.

❶ 모퉁이에 빵집이 있어요.

There is a bakery on the corner.

❷ 모퉁이에 버스 정류장이 있어요.

There is ______ on the corner.

❸ 모퉁이에 꽃가게가 있어요.

There is ______ on the corner.

2 I see ______ ______-ing . 나는 ~가 … 하는 것을 봐요.

❶ 나는 할머니가 손을 흔드는 것을 봐요.

I see Grandma waving .

❷ 나는 고양이 한 마리가 자고 있는 것을 봐요.

I see ______ ______ .

❸ 나는 개 한 마리가 짖고 있는 것을 봐요.

I see ______ ______ .

Word Box

- a flower shop 꽃가게
- a bus stop 버스 정류장
- hold the frog 개구리를 잡다
- a dog, bark 개 한 마리, 짖다
- a cat, sleep 고양이 한 마리, 자다
- climb the ladder 사다리를 오르다

3 I was afraid to ______ . 나는 ~하는 것이 무서웠어요.

❶ 나는 혼자 가는 것이 무서웠어요.

I was afraid to go alone .

❷ 나는 개구리를 잡는 것이 무서웠어요.

I was afraid to ______ .

❸ 나는 사다리를 오르는 것이 무서웠어요.

I was afraid to ______ .

Try Writing

배운 필수 문형을 활용해 영작해 보세요.

1

모퉁이에 벤치가 하나 있어요. (a bench)

______

2

나는 엄마가 운전하는 것을 봐요. (Mom, drive)

______

* 마지막 글자가 자음+e로 끝나는 동사는 e를 빼고 -ing를 붙여요.

3

나는 거미를 만지는 것이 무서웠어요. (touch the spider)

______

Think More

Reading a Map

★ 아이가 '도서관'을 찾아가려고 해요. 길 안내를 읽고 지도에서 도서관을 찾아보세요.

First, walk along **Oak Street**.
Then, turn left onto **Main Street**.
There are **maple trees** on the corner.
Turn right onto **Maple Street**.
Keep walking toward the **church**.
Across from the church, and you'll
find the **library**.

Plus 옛날에는 사람들이 직접 걸어 다니며 거리를 재고 지도를 그렸어요. 오늘날에는 인공위성과 위성사진을 이용해 훨씬 더 정밀한 지도를 만들 수 있어요. 위성이 찍은 사진을 보면 산, 강, 도로의 위치를 한눈에 알 수 있고, 컴퓨터가 이 사진들을 계산해 지도로 바꿔주기 때문에 작은 길까지도 자세히 확인할 수 있답니다.

Unit 7

Tim Learns the Rules

STEP 1 읽기 핵심 단어를 익혀서 스토리 듣고 읽기

STEP 2 이해 읽은 내용을 점검하여 스토리 이해하기

STEP 3 확장 필수 문형 학습으로 문장 이해력 키우기

Key Words

- 다음 단어들을 하나씩 손으로 짚으며 잘 들어 보세요. 37

rule

cafeteria

hallway

shout

bump into

pile

mess

stomachache

온라인 단어 학습

온라인 학습으로 단어를 꼼꼼히 익혀요.

A 단어와 우리말 뜻을 알맞게 연결하세요.

1	pile	• •	복통
2	cafeteria	• •	쌓다
3	bump into	• •	부딪히다
4	stomachache	• •	(학교) 식당

B 다음 우리말 뜻에 맞는 단어를 찾아 동그라미 하고 한 번 쓰세요.

h	d	o	m	r	i	a	s
a	j	b	z	f	u	p	h
l	t	r	y	v	i	k	o
l	a	q	m	e	s	s	u
w	e	f	w	c	t	d	t
a	p	r	u	l	e	x	g
y	h	y	k	w	j	u	o
q	c	g	s	r	n	x	b

1 소리치다

s

2 복도

h

3 규칙

r

4 엉망인 상태

m

Tim Learns the Rules

We hear the lunch bell.

The teacher says, “Class is over. It’s lunchtime.

Remember, **never** run or push others.

These rules help us enjoy lunch.”

over 끝이 난 | push 밀다 | others 다른 사람들 | enjoy 즐기다

We walk to the cafeteria.

But Tim runs down the hallway.

"I'm so hungry!" Tim shouts.

Tim bumps into his friends.

We wait in line for our food.

We only take as much as we can eat.

But Tim skips the line and goes first.

He piles on too much food.

wait in line 줄을 서서 기다리다 | as much as ~정도까지 많이

Tim eats too much, too fast.

His food makes a big mess.

Back in class, **Tim has** a stomachache.

The teacher says, "Tim, **this is why we** follow the rules."

back 돌아가서

Comprehension

A 보기에서 알맞은 단어를 골라 빈칸에 쓰세요.

wait bump rule hallway stomachache

1 

These ________s help us enjoy lunch.

2 

We ________ in line for our food.

3 

Back in class, Tim has a ________.

4 

Tim runs down the ________.

5 

Tim ________s into his friends.

B 들려주는 문장을 올바른 순서로 쓴 다음, 알맞은 그림에 번호를 쓰세요. (40)

1
wait in line	for our food.	we

→ ______________________

2
piles on	he	too much food.

→ ______________________

3
he	the hallway.	runs down

→ ______________________

C 다음 문장이 옳으면 T(True), 틀리면 F(False)에 동그라미 하세요.

1 Tim walks slowly to the cafeteria. T F

2 Tim skips the line. T F

3 Tim gets a headache. T F

D 다음을 읽고 올바른 행동은 'Dos' 칸에, 나쁜 행동은 'Don'ts' 칸에 기호를 쓰세요.

Dos(좋은 행동)	**Don'ts**(나쁜 행동)
Wait in line.	Skip the line.
Follow the rules.	Push others.

ⓐ Walk to the cafeteria.
ⓑ Make a mess.
ⓒ Bump into others.
ⓓ Pile on too much food.
ⓔ Take only as much as you can eat.
ⓕ Walk down the hallway.

Think & Say

이 글에 가장 알맞은 교훈에 ✓ 표시하세요 .

☐ Following the rules helps us enjoy lunch.
(규칙을 지키면 우리는 즐겁게 점심을 먹을 수 있어요.)

☐ Eating healthy food keeps us strong. (건강한 음식을 먹으면 튼튼해져요.)

☐ Sharing food with friends makes us happy. (친구들과 음식을 나눠 먹으면 행복해요.)

Listen Again

● 스토리를 다시 들으며 빈칸에 알맞은 단어를 써 넣으세요. 41

We hear the lunch bell. The teacher says, "Class is over. It's lunchtime. Remember, never run or ______ others. These ______s help us enjoy lunch."

We walk to the ______. But Tim runs down the ______. "I'm so hungry!" Tim ______s. Tim ______s into his friends.

We ______ in line for our food. We only take as much as we can eat. But Tim skips the line and goes first. He ______s on too much food.

Tim eats too much, too fast. His food makes a big ______.

Back in class, Tim has a ______. The teacher says, "Tim, this is why we follow the rules."

shout
pile
wait
push
hallway
rule
bump
mess
cafeteria
stomachache

Sentence Patterns

● 다음 필수 문형을 다양한 예문에 적용해 보세요. 42

1 Never ______ . 절대 ~하지 말아요.

❶ 절대 뛰거나 다른 사람들을 밀지 말아요.

Never run or push others.

❷ 절대 불장난하지 말아요.

Never ______ .

❸ 절대 음식을 낭비하지 말아요.

Never ______ .

2 He has ______ . 그는 ~가 있어요.

❶ 그는 복통이 있어요.

He has a stomachache.

❷ 그는 두통이 있어요.

He has ______ .

❸ 그는 열이 있어요.

He has ______ .

Word Box

- waste food 음식을 낭비하다
- play with fire 불장난하다
- a headache 두통
- a fever 열
- wear a coat 외투를 입다
- eat vegetables 채소를 먹다

3 This is why we ______ . 이것이 우리가 ~하는 이유예요.

❶ 이것이 우리가 규칙을 따르는 이유예요.

This is why we follow the rules .

❷ 이것이 우리가 채소를 먹는 이유예요.

This is why we ______ .

❸ 이것이 우리가 외투를 입는 이유예요.

This is why we ______ .

Try Writing

배운 필수 문형을 활용해 영작해 보세요.

1

절대 다른 사람들을 때리지 말아요. (hit others)

______

2

그는 감기에 걸렸어요. (a cold)

______

3

이것이 우리가 양치하는 이유예요. (brush our teeth)

______

Think More

School Cafeteria Rules

★ 빈칸에 알맞은 단어를 넣어 학교 식당에서 지켜야 하는 규칙을 완성하세요.

Wash your ______________ before eating.

Eat slowly and chew well.

Wait in ______________ for your food.

Take only as much as you can ______________.

Carry your ______________ carefully.

tray	line
eat	hands

Plus 세계 여러 나라의 학교 급식은 우리와 조금씩 달라요. 미국에서는 샌드위치, 피자, 햄버거 같은 음식이 우유나 과일과 함께 나와요. 프랑스에서는 코스 요리가 급식으로 나와서 샐러드, 메인 요리, 빵, 디저트까지 다양하게 즐길 수 있어요. 일본은 밥과 국, 반찬이 함께 나오며 때로는 도시락처럼 용기에 든 음식을 먹기도 해요.

Unit 8

A New Friend for Our Family

STEP 1 읽기 핵심 단어를 익혀서 스토리 듣고 읽기

STEP 2 이해 읽은 내용을 점검하여 스토리 이해하기

STEP 3 확장 필수 문형 학습으로 문장 이해력 키우기

Key Words

- 다음 단어들을 하나씩 손으로 짚으며 잘 들어 보세요. 43

meeting

quiet

clean

couch

change

turtle

move

welcome

온라인 단어 학습

온라인 학습으로 단어를 꼼꼼히 익혀요.

A 단어와 우리말 뜻을 알맞게 연결하세요.

1	welcome	거북
2	turtle	조용한
3	meeting	회의
4	quiet	환영하다

B 우리말 뜻에 맞는 단어가 되도록 빈칸에 알맞은 글자를 쓰세요.

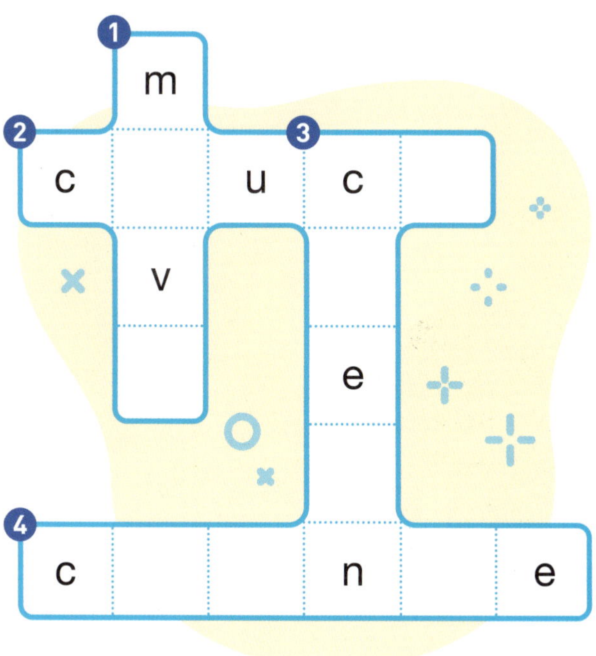

1 움직이다

2 긴 의자, 소파

3 깨끗한

4 바꾸다

A New Friend for Our Family

We're having a family meeting.

We want to get a new animal friend.

But everyone wants a different animal.

animal 동물 | everyone 모두 | different 다른

Dogs are playful and full of energy.

They like to play outside.

I'll walk my dog every day.

I love cats. They are quiet and clean.

They enjoy sleeping on the couch.

They are so cute.

playful 장난기 많은 | **walk** (동물을) 산책시키다

Fish are colorful and pretty.

It's important to keep their water clean.

I can change the water often.

Turtles are very calm.

They move slowly, so they don't need walks.

Turtles are a good choice for us.

colorful 알록달록한 | calm 차분한 | choice 선택

Every animal is special.

We want to welcome a good animal.

We'll love our new animal friend like family.

special 특별한

Comprehension

A 보기에서 알맞은 단어를 골라 빈칸에 쓰세요.

change   meeting   turtle   quiet   welcome

1 

_______s are a good choice for us.

2 

We want to _______ a good animal.

3 

We're having a family _______ .

4 

Cats are _______ and clean.

5 

I can _______ the water often.

B 들려주는 문장을 올바른 순서로 쓴 다음, 알맞은 그림에 번호를 쓰세요. 46

1
clean.	it's important	to keep their water

→

2
my dog	I'll walk	every day.

→

3
sleeping	on the couch.	they enjoy

→

C 다음 문장이 옳으면 T(True), 틀리면 F(False)에 동그라미 하세요.

1 This story is about a family meeting to get a dog. T F

2 Dogs don't need walks. T F

3 Turtles are playful and full of energy. T F

D 아래 문장을 읽고 각 동물의 특징과 돌보는 방법에 맞는 기호를 쓰세요.

	What are they like? (특징)	How do you take care of them? (돌보는 법)
		Walk them every day.
	quiet, clean	
	colorful, pretty	
		Keep their tank clean.

ⓐ calm, slow
ⓑ playful, full of energy
ⓒ Give them a cozy bed.
ⓓ Change the water often.

• cozy 아늑한

Think & Say

우리 가족이 반려동물을 키운다면 어떤 동물이 좋을까요?
하나를 골라 보세요.

- ☐ dog
- ☐ cat
- ☐ fish
- ☐ turtle
- ☐ parrot
- ☐ ________

I want a/an ________
because ________.

Listen Again

● 스토리를 다시 들으며 빈칸에 알맞은 단어를 써 넣으세요. 47

We're having a family ______. We want to get a new animal friend. But everyone wants a ______ animal.

Dogs are playful and full of energy. They like to play outside. I'll ______ my dog every day.
I love cats. They are ______ and clean. They enjoy sleeping on the ______. They are so cute.

Fish are colorful and pretty. It's important to keep their water ______. I can ______ the water often.
______s are very calm. They move slowly, so they don't need walks. Turtles are a good choice for us.

Every animal is ______. We want to ______ a good animal. We'll love our new animal friend like family.

couch
quiet
special
walk
clean
turtle
welcome
change
meeting
different

Sentence Patterns

● 다음 필수 문형을 다양한 예문에 적용해 보세요. 48

1 They like to ______. 그들은 ~하는 것을 좋아해요.

① 그들은 밖에서 노는 것을 좋아해요.

They like to play outside.

② 그들은 침대에서 뛰는 것을 좋아해요.

They like to ______.

③ 그들은 함께 춤추는 것을 좋아해요.

They like to ______.

2 I will ______. 나는 ~할 거예요.

① 나는 내 개를 산책시킬 거예요.

I will walk my dog.

② 나는 내 방을 청소할 거예요.

I will ______.

③ 나는 물고기에게 먹이를 줄 거예요.

I will ______.

Word Box

- jump on the bed 침대에서 뛰다
- say thank you 고맙다고 말하다
- dance together 함께 춤추다
- feed the fish 물고기에게 먹이를 주다
- clean my room 내 방을 청소하다
- help others 다른 사람을 돕다

3 It's important to ______ . ~하는 것이 중요해요.

① 물을 깨끗하게 유지하는 것이 중요해요.

It's important to keep their water clean .

② 다른 사람을 돕는 것이 중요해요.

It's important to ______ .

③ 고맙다고 말하는 것이 중요해요.

It's important to ______ .

Try Writing

배운 필수 문형을 활용해 영작해 보세요.

1

나는 꽃에 물을 줄 거예요. (water the flowers)

______

2

그들은 당근 먹는 것을 좋아해요. (eat carrots)

______

3

일찍 자는 것이 중요해요. (sleep early)

______

Think More

Taking Care of Pets

★ 반려동물을 키울 때 무엇이 필요할까요? 빈칸에 알맞은 단어를 찾아 쓰세요.

Pets need healthy ____________.

Pets need clean ____________ to drink.

Pets need a quiet and safe place to ____________.

Pets need to exercise every day.

love	rest
food	water

Pets need ____________ and kindness.

Plus 반려동물은 우리의 친구이자 함께 살아가는 가족이에요. 매일 밥을 챙겨 주고, 아플 때는 병원에 데려가는 것도 우리의 몫이지요. 평생 동안 사랑과 관심으로 잘 돌보겠다는 책임감을 가질 때, 반려동물도 행복하고 우리도 진정한 가족의 기쁨을 느낄 수 있답니다.

Review Test 2
(Unit ⑤ – Unit ⑧)

/ 25개

A 그림에 알맞은 단어를 고르세요.

1 

ⓐ move ⓑ wave ⓒ shout

2 

ⓐ pile ⓑ mess ⓒ slice

3 

ⓐ couch ⓑ fence ⓒ map

4 

ⓐ afraid ⓑ quiet ⓒ clean

5 

ⓐ change ⓑ share ⓒ spread

6 

ⓐ across ⓑ spooky ⓒ right

B 그림을 보고 알맞은 문장을 고르세요.

1 

ⓐ Let's make Halloween toast!

ⓑ All the spooky toast is ready!

2 

ⓐ Tim piles on too much food.

ⓑ Tim bumps into his friends.

3 

ⓐ The house has a red fence.

ⓑ The house has a green door.

4 

ⓐ We're having a family meeting.

ⓑ We like to play outside.

★★
C 알맞은 단어를 골라 문장을 완성하세요.

1 Grandma's house is ⓐ near ⓑ under the big park.

2 We're ⓐ go ⓑ going to make fun monster faces.

3 Cats ⓐ enjoy ⓑ enjoys sleeping on the couch.

4 Back in class, Tim ⓐ has ⓑ have a stomachache.

D 짧은 글을 읽고 질문에 알맞은 대답을 고르세요.

1 다음 설명을 참고해 알맞은 토스트를 고르세요.

First, spread cream cheese on a slice of toast. Next, make a fun face with olives. Now it looks like a ghost!

ⓐ 

ⓑ 

2 다음 글을 읽고, They가 가리키는 대상을 고르세요.

They are very calm.
They move slowly.
They don't need walks.

ⓐ turtles ⓑ dogs

3 빈칸에 들어갈 알맞은 단어를 고르세요.

The teacher says, "It's lunchtime. Remember, never run or push others. These ________ help us enjoy lunch."

ⓐ games ⓑ rules

4 빈칸에 들어갈 알맞은 단어를 고르세요.

I'm going to Grandma's house on my own. This __________ will help me find the way.

ⓐ map ⓑ couch

E 필수 패턴을 활용해 우리말에 알맞은 영어 문장을 완성하세요.

I was afraid to ______.
This is why we ______.
They like to ______.
We're going to ______.

1 우리는 달걀을 살 거예요.

→ ______________________ buy some eggs.

2 이것이 우리가 채소를 먹는 이유예요.

→ ______________________ eat vegetables.

3 그들은 함께 춤추는 것을 좋아해요.

→ ______________________ dance together.

4 나는 개구리를 잡는 것이 무서웠어요.

→ ______________________ hold the frog.

F 우리말에 알맞은 영어 문장을 쓰세요.

1 다른 사람을 돕는 것이 중요해요. (help, it's, others, to, important)

→ ______________________________________.

2 나는 내 방을 청소할 거예요. (will, my room, clean, I)

→ ______________________________________.

3 나는 고양이 한 마리가 자고 있는 것을 봐요. (a cat, I, sleeping, see)

→ ______________________________________.

A권이 끝났습니다.
B권으로 넘어갈까요?

저자 C2 Archive (대표 Olene Kim)

지난 20여 년간 영어라는 언어를 어린이들이 어려움 없이 단계적으로 습득해갈 수 있도록 효과적인 교수법을 연구하여 다양한 교재로 구현해 온 영어교육 전문 집필진입니다. 파닉스, 리딩, 코스북, 문법 등 여러 분야의 ELT 교재와 영어 단행본 학습서를 집필·개발하였습니다.

저자 기적학습연구소

"혼자서 작은 산을 넘는 아이가 나중에 큰 산도 넘습니다." 본 연구소는 아이들이 혼자서 큰 산까지 넘을 수 있는 힘을 키워주고자 합니다. 아이들의 연령에 맞게 학습의 산을 작게 만들어 혼자서도 쉽게 넘을 수 있게 만듭니다. 때로는 작은 고난도 경험하게 하여 성취감도 맛보게 합니다. 그리고 아이들에게 실제로 적용해서 검증을 통해 차근차근 책을 만듭니다.

기적의 영어리딩 Level 3A

Miracle Series – Reading English

초판 발행 • 2025년 11월 15일

지은이 • C2 Archive, 기적학습연구소

발행인 • 이종원
발행처 • (주)길벗스쿨
출판사 등록일 • 2025년 5월 28일 | **주소** • 서울시 마포구 월드컵로 10길 56(서교동)
대표 전화 • 02)332-0931 | **팩스** • 02)310-4700
홈페이지 • www.gilbutschool.co.kr | **이메일** • gilbut@gilbut.co.kr

담당편집 • 김소이(soykim@gilbut.co.kr), 이경희, 김예지 | **기획** • 이경희, 김남희, 박민혜 | **표지디자인** • 이현숙 | **제작** • 손일순
영업마케팅 • 문세연, 박선경, 구혜지, 박다슬 | **웹마케팅** • 박달님, 이재윤, 이지수, 나혜연 | **영업관리** • 정경화 | **독자지원** • 윤정아

교정교열 • 최주연 | **전산편집** • 기본기획 | **본문디자인** • 신세진 | **삽화** • 강나래, 삼식이, 엄수지, 윤지현, 이탁근, 조은, 최선화, Bananabee | **영문 감수** • Ryan P. Lagace
인쇄 및 제본 • 영림 | **녹음** • 아람 멀티미디어

ISBN 979-11-7467-057-1 64740 (길벗 도서번호 30636)
정가 17,000원

기적 영어 학습서

기본이 탄탄! 실전에서 척척!
유초등 필수 영어능력을 길러주는 코어 학습서

유아 영어

재미있는 액티비티가 가득한
4~6세를 위한 영어 워크북

4세 이상 | 5세 이상 | 6세 이상 | 6세 이상

파닉스 완성 프로그램

알파벳 음가 → 사이트워드
→ 읽기 연습까지!
리딩을 위한 탄탄한 기초 만들기

6세 이상 전 3권 | 1~3학년 | 1~3학년 전 3권

영어 단어

영어 실력의 가장 큰 바탕은 어휘력!
교과과정 필수 어휘 익히기

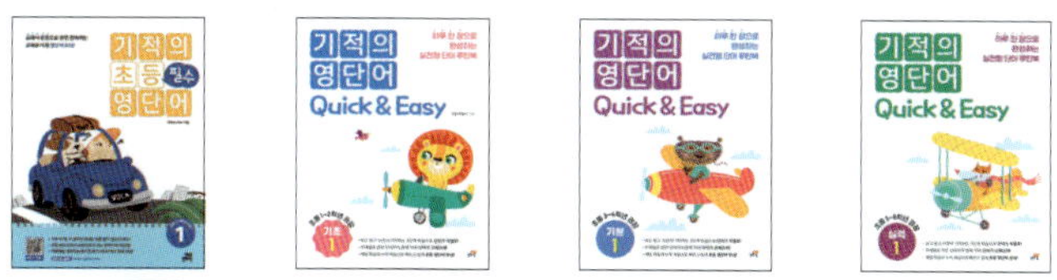

3학년 이상 전 2권 | 1~2학년 전 2권 | 3~4학년 전 2권 | 5~6학년 전 2권

영어 리딩

패턴 문장 리딩으로 시작해
정확한 해석을 위한 끊어 읽기까지!
탄탄한 독해 실력 쌓기

2~3학년 전 3권 | 3~4학년 전 3권 | 4~5학년 전 2권 | 5~6학년 전 2권 | 5~6학년 전 2권

영어 라이팅

저학년은 패턴 영작으로,
고학년은 5형식 문장 만들기 연습으로
튼튼한 영작 실력 완성

2학년 이상 전 4권 | 4학년 이상 전 5권 | 5학년 이상 전 2권 | 6학년 이상

영어일기

한 줄 쓰기부터 생활일기,
주제일기까지!
영어 글쓰기 실력을 키우는 시리즈

3학년 이상 | 4~5학년 | 5~6학년

영문법

중학 영어 대비, 영어 구사
정확성을 키워주는 영문법 학습

4~5학년 전 2권 | 5~6학년 전 3권 | 6학년 이상

초등 필수 영어 무작정 따라하기

초등 시기에 놓쳐서는 안 될 필수 학습은 바로 영어 교과서!
영어 교과서 5종의 핵심 내용을 쏙쏙 뽑아 한 권으로 압축 정리했습니다.
초등 과정의 필수학습으로 기초를 다져서 중학교 및 상위 학습의 단단한 토대가 되게 합니다.

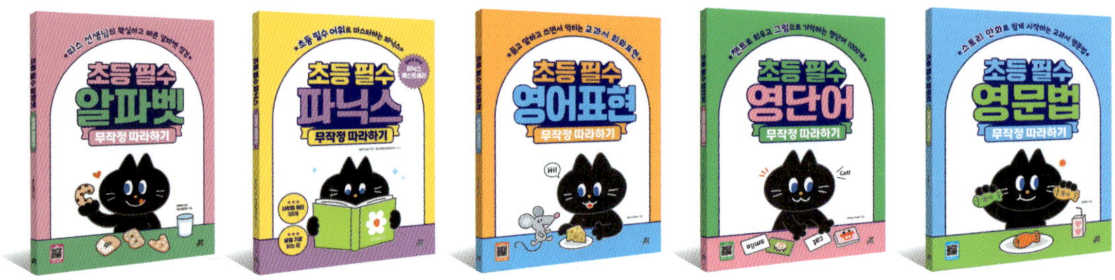

1~2학년 | 2~3학년 | 2~3학년 | 3학년 이상 | 4학년 이상

미국교과서 리딩

문제의 차이가 영어 실력의 차이! 논픽션 리딩에 강해지는 《미국교과서 READING》
논픽션 리딩에 가장 좋은 재료인 미국 교과과정의 주제를 담은 지문을 읽고, 독해력과
문제 해결력을 두루 향상시킬 수 있도록 구성한 단계별 리딩 프로그램

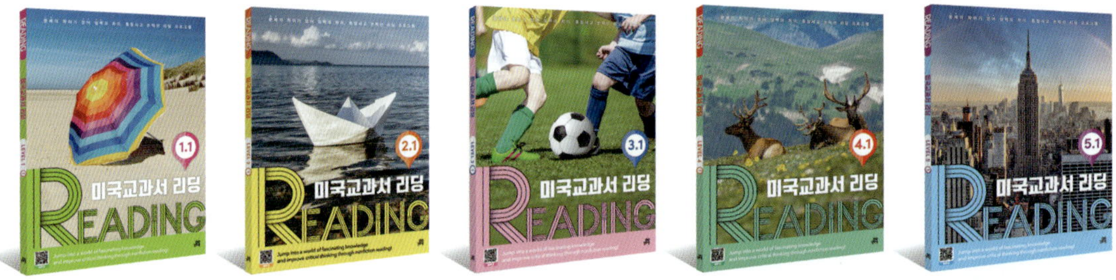

- LEVEL 1 준비 단계
- LEVEL 2 시작 단계
- LEVEL 3 정독 연습 단계
- LEVEL 4 독해 정확성 향상 단계
- LEVEL 5 독해 통합심화 단계

3A

90~110 words
AR 1.3~2.3

기적의 영어리딩

with 문장 패턴

Practice Book

(정답과 해석 포함)

길벗스쿨

3A

기적의 영어리딩

Practice Book

Unit 1 The Best Birthday Ever!

READ AND WRITE 문장을 의미 단위로 나눠 읽은 뒤, 전체 문장을 따라 쓰세요.

1 내 생일이 곧 다가와요!

My birthday	is coming	soon!
내 생일이	다가오고 있다	곧

2 나는 파티를 위한 초대장을 만들어요.

I	make	invitations	for the party.
나는	만든다	초대장들을	파티를 위한

3 나는 내 친구들에게 초대장을 줘요.

I	give	the invitations	to my friends.
나는	준다	초대장들을	내 친구들에게

4 아빠는 풍선으로 방을 꾸며요.

Dad	decorates	the room	with balloons.
아빠는	꾸민다	방을	풍선들로

5 엄마는 쿠키와 컵케이크를 구워요.

Mom	bakes	cookies and cupcakes.
엄마는	굽는다	쿠키와 컵케이크를

6 선물들이 젖을까요?

Will ~일까요?	the presents 선물들이	get wet? 젖다

7 비가 내 파티를 망치게 될까요?

Will ~일까요?	the rain 비가	mess up 망친다	my party? 내 파티를

8 나는 초인종이 울리는 소리가 들려요.

I 나는	hear 듣는다	the doorbell 초인종이	ring. 울리는 것을

9 파티가 끝난 후, 우리는 빗속에서 아주 재미있게 놀아요.

After the party, 파티가 끝난 후	We 우리는	have so much fun 아주 즐겁게 보낸다	in the rain. 빗속에서

10 이것은 최고의 생일이에요!

This is 이것은 ~이다	the best birthday 최고의 생일	ever! 지금까지

Unit 2

Leo Gets Sick

READ AND WRITE 문장을 의미 단위로 나눠 읽은 뒤, 전체 문장을 따라 쓰세요.

1 레오는 밖에서 노는 것을 매우 좋아해요.

Leo	loves	playing	outside.
레오는	매우 좋아한다	노는 것을	밖에서

2 하지만 레오는 씻는 것을 건너뛰어요.

But	Leo	skips	washing.
하지만	레오는	건너뛴다	씻는 것을

3 레오는 더러운 손으로 먹어요.

Leo	eats	with his dirty hands.
레오는	먹는다	그의 더러운 손으로

4 세균들이 그의 샌드위치와 유리잔에 묻어요.

Germs	get on	his sandwich and glass.
세균들이	묻는다	그의 샌드위치와 유리잔에

5 그날 오후, 레오의 코에서 콧물이 흐르기 시작해요.

That afternoon,	Leo's nose	starts running.
그날 오후	레오의 코가	흐르기 시작한다

6 엄마는 레오를 의사 선생님에게 데려가요.

Mom 엄마는	takes 데려간다	Leo 레오를	to the doctor. 의사 선생님에게

7 세균들은 너를 아프게 만들 수 있어.

Germs 세균들은	can make 만들 수 있다	you 너를	sick. 아프게

8 이 건강 습관들을 따라 주렴.

Please 부디 ~해 주세요	follow 따른다	these healthy habits. 이 건강 습관들을

9 집에서 레오는 비누로 손을 씻어요.

At home, 집에서	Leo washes 레오는 씻는다	his hands 그의 손을	with soap. 비누로

10 이제 레오는 매일 의사 선생님의 조언을 따라요!

Now, 이제	Leo follows 레오는 따른다	the doctor's advice 의사 선생님의 조언을	every day! 매일

Unit 3 Hello! We Are Signs

READ AND WRITE 문장을 의미 단위로 나눠 읽은 뒤, 전체 문장을 따라 쓰세요.

1 우리는 박물관에 있는 "하지 마세요" 표지판들이에요.

We are	some "do not" signs	in museums.
우리는 ~이다	"하지 마세요" 표지판들	박물관에

2 우리에 대해 알고 싶나요?

Do you want	to learn	about us?
원하나요?	알기를	우리에 대해

3 어떤 물건들은 쉽게 깨질 수 있어요.

Some things	can break	easily.
어떤 물건들은	깨질 수 있다	쉽게

4 안에서 뛰는 것은 위험할 수 있어요.

Running inside	can be	dangerous.
안에서 뛰는 것은	~일 수 있다	위험한

5 음식을 가져오거나 안에서 먹지 마세요.

Don't	bring or eat food	inside.
하지 마세요	음식을 가져오거나 먹는다	안에서

6 음식은 지저분하게 만들 수 있어요.

Food 음식은	can make 만들 수 있다	a mess. 엉망진창을

7 (카메라) 플래시는 미술품을 손상시킬 수 있어요.

Flash (카메라) 플래시는	can damage 손상시킬 수 있다	art. 미술품을

8 우리는 박물관을 안전하게 지키는 데 도움이 돼요.

We 우리는	help 돕는다	keep museums 박물관을 지키는 것을	safe. 안전하게

9 규칙들을 따르는 것을 기억하세요.

Remember 기억하세요	to follow 따르는 것을	the rules. 규칙들을

10 우리의 말을 들어줘서 고마워요.

Thank you 고마워요	for listening 들어줘서	to us. 우리를

Unit 4 The Rainbow Garden

READ AND WRITE 문장을 의미 단위로 나눠 읽은 뒤, 전체 문장을 따라 쓰세요.

1 미아는 그림을 그리고 있어요.

Mia 미아는	is painting 그리고 있다	a picture. 그림을

2 그녀는 큰 종이를 노란색으로 칠해요.

She 그녀는	paints 칠한다	her big paper 그녀의 큰 종이를	yellow. 노란색으로

3 아름다운 노란 정원이 될 거야.

It 그것은	will be ~이 될 것이다	a beautiful yellow garden. 아름다운 노란 정원

4 루나는 빨간 물감에 손을 담가요.

Luna 루나는	dips 담근다	her hand 그녀의 손을	in red paint. 빨간 물감에

5 그녀는 노란 그림에 그것을 찍어요.

She 그녀는	stamps 찍는다	it 그것을 (= 그녀의 손을)	on the yellow picture. 노란 그림에

6 그녀는 그것을 파란 물감에 담가요.

She	dips	it	in blue paint.
그녀는	담근다	그것을 (= 그녀의 손을)	파란 물감에

7 그녀는 루나의 두 손을 서로 문질러요.

She	rubs	both of Luna's hands	together.
그녀는	문지른다	루나의 두 손을	함께

8 이제 물감이 보라색으로 변해요!

Now,	the paint	turns	purple!
이제	물감이	변한다	보라색으로

9 루나, 여기에 손자국을 찍어 봐!

Luna,	stamp	your hands	here!
루나	찍어라	너의 손을	여기에

10 그들은 함께 미소 짓고 웃어요.

They	smile and laugh	together.
그들은	미소 짓고 웃는다	함께

Unit 5 Spooky Halloween Toast

READ AND WRITE 문장을 의미 단위로 나눠 읽은 뒤, 전체 문장을 따라 쓰세요.

1 핼러윈 토스트를 만들자!

Let's	make	Halloween Toast!
~하자	만든다	핼러윈 토스트를

2 우리는 재미있는 괴물 얼굴을 만들 거예요.

We're going to	make	fun	monster faces.
우리는 ~할 것이다	만든다	재미있는	괴물 얼굴들을

3 이것들은 만들기 쉽고 재미있어요.

These are	easy and fun	to make.
이것들은 ~이다	쉽고 재미있는	만들기에

4 먼저, 토스트 한 조각에 아보카도를 펴 바르세요.

First,	spread	avocado	on a slice of toast.
먼저	펴 바르세요	아보카도를	토스트 한 조각 위에

5 다음으로, 눈을 만들기 위해 올리브를 올리세요.

Next,	add	olives	for the eyes.
다음으로	추가하세요	올리브를	눈을 (만들기) 위해

6 다음으로, 바나나를 반으로 자르세요.

Next,	cut	a banana	in half.
다음으로	자르세요	바나나를	반으로

7 다음으로, 올리브로 재미있는 얼굴을 만들어 보세요.

Next,	make	a fun face	with olives.
다음으로	만드세요	재미있는 얼굴을	올리브로

8 이제 유령처럼 보여요!

Now	it	looks like	a ghost!
이제	그것은	~처럼 보인다	유령

9 다음으로, 치즈 조각들을 붕대처럼 올리세요.

Next,	add	cheese strips	like bandages.
다음으로	추가하세요	치즈 조각들을	붕대처럼

10 가족과 친구들과 함께 토스트를 나누어 먹어요.

Share	the toast	with your family and friends.
나누세요	토스트를	가족과 친구들과 함께

Unit 6 A Trip to Grandma's House

READ AND WRITE 문장을 의미 단위로 나눠 읽은 뒤, 전체 문장을 따라 쓰세요.

1 나는 혼자서 할머니 댁에 갈 거예요.

I'm going	to Grandma's house	on my own.
나는 갈 것이다	할머니 댁에	혼자서

2 이 지도는 내가 길을 찾는 데 도와줄 거예요.

This map	will help	me	find the way.
이 지도는	도와줄 것이다	나를	길을 찾도록

3 할머니 댁은 큰 공원 근처에 있어요.

Grandma's house	is	near the big park.
할머니 댁은	~에 있다	큰 공원에서 가까이

4 먼저, 나는 오크 거리를 따라 걸어요.

First,	I	walk	along Oak Street.
먼저	나는	걷는다	오크 거리를 따라서

5 그다음, 메인 거리로 오른쪽으로 돌아요.

Then,	I	turn right	onto Main Street.
그다음	나는	오른쪽으로 돈다	메인 거리로

6 모퉁이에 빵집이 있어요.

There is ~이 있다	a bakery 빵집	on the corner. 모퉁이에

7 할머니 댁에는 초록색 문이 있어요.

Her house 그녀의 집은	has 가지고 있다	a green door. 초록색 문을

8 창문에서 할머니가 손을 흔드는 게 보여요.

I see 나는 본다	Grandma 할머니가	waving 손 흔드는 것을	from her window. 창문에서

9 처음에는 혼자 가는 것이 무서웠어요.

At first, 처음에는	I was afraid 나는 무서웠다	to go 가기에	alone. 혼자

10 할머니 댁에 또 가고 싶어 너무 기대돼요!

I 나는	can't wait 기다릴 수 없다(= 너무 기대된다)	to visit Grandma 할머니 댁에 가는 것을	again! 다시

Unit 7 Tim Learns the Rules

READ AND WRITE 문장을 의미 단위로 나눠 읽은 뒤, 전체 문장을 따라 쓰세요.

1 기억하세요, 절대 뛰거나 다른 사람들을 밀지 마세요.

Remember, 기억하세요	never 절대 ~마세요	run or push others. 뛰거나 다른 사람들을 민다

2 이 규칙들은 우리가 즐겁게 점심을 먹도록 도와줘요.

These rules 이 규칙들은	help 도와준다	us 우리를	enjoy lunch. 즐겁게 점심을 먹도록

3 하지만 팀은 복도를 달려가요.

But 하지만	Tim 팀은	runs 달린다	down the hallway. 복도를 따라

4 팀은 그의 친구들과 부딪혀요.

Tim 팀은	bumps into 부딪힌다	his friends. 그의 친구들과

5 우리는 줄을 서서 음식을 기다려요.

We 우리는	wait 기다린다	in line 줄을 서서	for our food. 음식을 (받기) 위해

6 우리는 먹을 수 있는 만큼만 가져가요.

We 우리는	only take 오직 가져간다	as much as ~만큼	we can eat. 우리가 먹을 수 있는

7 하지만 팀은 줄을 건너뛰고 먼저 가요.

But 하지만	Tim 팀은	skips the line 줄을 건너뛴다	and goes first. 그리고 먼저 간다

8 그는 음식을 너무 많이 쌓아 올려요.

He 그는	piles on 쌓는다	too much food. 너무 많은 음식을

9 팀은 너무 많이, 너무 빨리 먹어요.

Tim 팀은	eats 먹는다	too much, 너무 많이	too fast. 너무 빨리

10 팀, 이래서 우리가 규칙을 지키는 거란다.

Tim, 팀	this is why 이것이 이유다	we follow 우리가 따르는	the rules. 규칙들을

Unit 8 A New Friend for Our Family

READ AND WRITE 문장을 의미 단위로 나눠 읽은 뒤, 전체 문장을 따라 쓰세요.

1 우리는 새 동물 친구를 키우고 싶어요.

We	want	to get	a new animal friend.
우리는	원한다	갖기를	새 동물 친구를

2 하지만 모두 다른 동물을 원해요.

But	everyone	wants	a different animal.
하지만	모든 사람이	원한다	다른 동물을

3 그들은 밖에서 노는 것을 좋아해요.

They	like	to play	outside.
그들은	좋아한다	노는 것을	밖에서

4 나는 매일 개를 산책시킬 거예요.

I'll	walk	my dog	every day.
나는 ~할 것이다	산책시킨다	내 개를	매일

5 그들은 소파에서 자는 것을 좋아해요.

They	enjoy	sleeping	on the couch.
그들은	즐긴다	자는 것을	소파에서

6 물을 깨끗하게 유지하는 것이 중요해요.

It's important 중요하다	to keep 유지하는 것이	their water 그들의 물을	clean. 깨끗하게

7 나는 자주 물을 갈아줄 수 있어요.

I 나는	can change 갈아줄 수 있다	the water 물을	often. 자주

8 거북은 우리에게 좋은 선택이에요.

Turtles are 거북은 ~이다	a good choice 좋은 선택	for us. 우리에게

9 우리는 좋은 동물을 맞이하고 싶어요.

We want 우리는 원한다	to welcome 환영하기를	a good animal. 좋은 동물을

10 새 동물 친구를 가족처럼 사랑할 거예요.

We'll 우리는 ~할 것이다	love 사랑한다	our new animal friend 우리의 새 동물 친구를	like family. 가족처럼

GOOD
JOB

3A

기적의 영어리딩

Answer Key

Unit 1

The Best Birthday Ever!

최고의 생일

Key Words

birthday 생일	**invitation** 초대장, 초대	**party** 파티	**decorate** 장식하다
balloon 풍선	**rain** 비가 오다	**present** 선물	**umbrella** 우산

Sentence Patterns

• **I can't wait for ______!**	나는 ~가 너무 기다려져요!
• **It starts to ______.**	~하기 시작해요.
• **This is the best ______ ever!**	이것은 최고의 ~예요!

Story Reading

p.14

내 생일이 곧 다가와요!
나는 9살이 돼요.
나는 파티를 위한 초대장을 만들어요.

잭의 아홉 번째 생일파티
3월 15일 일요일 오후 5시
잭의 집, 레인보우 거리 426
놀러 와서 재미있게 놀자!

나는 내 친구들에게 초대장을 줘요.
나는 그 파티가 너무 기다려져요!

p.15

드디어 파티 날이에요!
아빠는 풍선으로 방을 꾸며요.
엄마는 쿠키와 컵케이크를 구워요.

내 남동생은 식탁 위에 간식을 놓아요.
모든 것이 준비되었어요.

p.16

오, 안 돼! 비가 오기 시작해요.
내 친구들이 올까요?

선물들이 비에 젖을까요?

비가 내 파티를 망치게 될까요?

p.17

그때, 초인종 소리가 들려요.
내 친구들이 우산을 들고 환하게 웃으며 여기 와 있어요.

파티가 끝난 후, 우리는 빗속에서 아주 재미있게 놀아요.
"이건 최고의 생일이야!"

Answers

p.13

A 단어와 우리말 뜻을 알맞게 연결하세요.

1. invitation – 초대장, 초대
2. party – 파티
3. present – 선물
4. birthday – 생일

B 다음 우리말 뜻에 맞는 단어를 찾아 동그라미 하고 한 번 쓰세요.

u	m	b	r	e	l	l	a
s	i	p	b	l	m	k	g
n	t	y	a	r	a	i	n
p	o	f	l	e	h	b	x
h	e	s	l	g	d	k	a
k	v	h	o	l	j	n	i
d	e	c	o	r	a	t	e
w	y	i	n	u	k	c	w

1. 장식하다 decorate
2. 풍선 balloon
3. 비가 오다 rain
4. 우산 umbrella

Unit 1 13

p.18 Comprehension

A 보기에서 알맞은 단어를 골라 빈칸에 쓰세요.

snack invitation balloon birthday present

1. My birthday is coming soon!
2. I give the invitations to my friends.
3. Dad decorates the room with balloons.
4. Will the presents get wet?
5. My brother puts the snacks on the table.

18

p.19

B 들려주는 문장을 올바른 순서로 쓴 다음, 알맞은 그림에 번호를 쓰세요.

1. so much fun / in the rain. / we have
→ We have so much fun in the rain.
2. invitations / I make / for the party.
→ I make invitations for the party.
3. Mom / cookies and cupcakes. / bakes
→ Mom bakes cookies and cupcakes.

2 3 1

C 다음 문장이 옳으면 T(True), 틀리면 F(False)에 동그라미 하세요.

1. Jack is turning 10 on his birthday. — F
2. Mom bakes cookies and cupcakes. — T
3. After the party, the children play in the rain. — T

Unit 1 19

p.20

D 주인공의 기분이 어떻게 변했는지 보고, 알맞은 단어에 동그라미 하세요.

My birthday is coming soon! I'm (excited / sad). → excited
It starts to rain. I'm (happy / worried). → worried
My friends are here. I'm (surprised / sorry). → surprised
We have so much fun in the rain. We're (happy / tired). → happy

• excited 신이 난 surprised 놀란 worried 걱정하는 tired 피곤한

Think & Say

생일에 내가 가장 좋아하는 활동은 무엇인가요?

- making a wish
- eating cake
- blowing out the candles
- having fun with friends

The best part of my birthday is ______.

내 생일에서 가장 좋은 건 ______야.

20

p.21 Listen Again

• 스토리를 다시 들으며 빈칸에 알맞은 단어를 써 넣으세요.

My birthday is coming soon! I'm turning 9. I make invitations for the party.
I give the invitations to my friends. I can't wait for the party!

Finally, it's party day! Dad decorates the room with balloons. Mom bakes cookies and cupcakes.
My brother puts the snacks on the table.
Everything is ready.

Oh no! It starts to rain. Will my friends come?
Will the presents get wet? Will the rain mess up my party?

Then, I hear the doorbell ring. My friends are here with umbrellas and big smiles.
After the party, we have so much fun in the rain. "This is the best birthday ever!"

decorate fun invitation party birthday snack present balloon umbrella rain

Unit 1 21

p.22 Sentence Patterns

• 다음 필수 문형을 다양한 예문에 적용해 보세요.

1 I can't wait for ______!

- 나는 그 파티가 너무 기다려져요! I can't wait for the party!
- 나는 그 소풍이 너무 기다려져요! I can't wait for the picnic!
- 나는 그 공연이 너무 기다려져요! I can't wait for the concert!

2 It starts to ______. ~하기 시작해요.

- 비가 오기 시작해요. It starts to rain.
- 눈이 오기 시작해요. It starts to snow.
- 천둥이 치기 시작해요. It starts to thunder.

Word Box: •present 선물 •the concert 그 공연 •the picnic 그 소풍 •trip 여행 •snow 눈이 오다 •thunder 천둥이 치다

22

p.23

3 This is the best ______ ever!

- 이것은 최고의 생일이에요! This is the best birthday ever!
- 이것은 최고의 선물이에요! This is the best present ever!
- 이것은 최고의 여행이에요! This is the best trip ever!

Try Writing 배운 필수 문형을 활용해 영작해 보세요.

1. 나는 그 방학이 너무 기다려져요! (the vacation)
I can't wait for the vacation!
2. 바람이 불기 시작해요. (get windy)
It starts to get windy.
3. 이것은 최고의 케이크예요! (cake)
This is the best cake ever!

Unit 1 23

p.24 Think More

Chad's Birthday Invitation

★ 다음을 참고하여 생일파티 초대장을 완성하세요.

Whose birthday? Chad
When? July 8, 3 o'clock
Where? Chad's house

Come to Chad's Birthday Party!
Date: Saturday, (July) (8)
Time: (3) p.m.
Place: Chad's (house)
21 Rose Street, Garden Town.
There will be cake, games, and fun!

24

채드의 생일 초대장

채드의 생일파티에 와!
• 날짜: 7월 8일 토요일
• 시간: 오후 3시
• 장소: 채드의 집
가든타운 로즈 거리 21

케이크와 게임, 재미있는 놀거리가 있을 거야!

Unit 2

Leo Gets Sick

레오가 아파요

Key Words

dirt 흙	**wash** 씻다	**nose** 코	**sick** 아픈
doctor 의사	**germ** 세균	**healthy** 건강한	**soap** 비누

Sentence Patterns

• **He loves ______ -ing .**	그는 ~하는 것을 매우 좋아해요.
• **Mom takes ______ to ______ .**	엄마는 ~을 …에 데려가요.
• **They can make you ______ .**	그것들은 너를 ~하게 만들 수 있어.

Story Reading

p.28

레오는 밖에서 노는 것을 매우 좋아해요.
그는 마당을 뛰어다니며 흙을 파요.

점심시간에 엄마가 말해요. "손을 씻으렴!"
하지만 레오는 손 씻기를 건너뛰어요.
"나중에 할게요." 레오가 말해요.

get sick: 병에 걸리다

p.29

레오는 더러운 손으로 먹어요.
세균들이 그의 샌드위치와 유리잔에 묻어요.

그날 오후, 레오의 코에서 콧물이 흐르기 시작해요.
목도 아파요.
"나 왜 아픈 거지?" 레오는 궁금해요.

p.30

엄마는 레오를 의사 선생님에게 데려가요.
의사 선생님이 말해요. "세균들이 너를 아프게 할 수 있어.
이 건강 습관들을 따라 주렴."

· 손을 자주 씻어요
· 건강한 음식을 먹어요
· 기침할 때 입을 가려요
· 물을 많이 마셔요
· 충분히 쉬어요

p.31

집에서 레오는 비누로 손을 씻어요.
"이거 쉽잖아!" 레오가 말해요.
이제 레오는 매일 의사 선생님의 조언을 따라요!

Answers

p.27

A 단어와 우리말 뜻을 알맞게 연결하세요.

1 doctor, 2 healthy, 3 germ, 4 soap — 아픈 / 세균 / 건강한 / 의사

B 우리말 뜻에 맞는 단어가 되도록 빈칸에 알맞은 글자를 쓰세요.

s i c k / d i r t / w a s h / n o s e

1 아픈 2 흙 3 씻다 4 코

p.32 Comprehension

A 보기에서 알맞은 단어를 골라 빈칸에 쓰세요.

dirty soap outside sick germ

1. Leo loves playing outside.
2. The doctor says, "Germs can make you sick."
3. "Why do I feel sick?" Leo wonders.
4. Leo eats with his dirty hands.
5. Leo washes his hands with soap.

p.33

B 들려주는 문장을 올바른 순서로 쓴 다음, 알맞은 그림에 번호를 쓰세요.

1. starts / his nose / running. → His nose starts running.
2. takes him / to the doctor. / Mom → Mom takes him to the doctor.
3. in the dirt. / he / digs → He digs in the dirt.

3 / 1 / 2

C 다음 문장이 맞으면 T(True), 틀리면 F(False)에 동그라미 하세요.

1. This story is about making a sandwich. — F
2. Leo washes his hands before eating lunch. — F
3. Leo says washing his hands is easy. — T

p.34

D 아래 문장들을 잘 읽고, 원인과 결과가 되도록 빈칸에 알맞은 기호를 쓰세요.

Cause(원인)	Effect(결과)
ⓑ	Leo's nose starts running. His throat hurts.
Leo feels sick.	ⓐ
The doctor gives him advice.	ⓒ

ⓐ Mom takes Leo to the doctor.
ⓑ Leo eats with his dirty hands.
ⓒ Leo starts washing his hands every day.

Think & Say 이 글에서 가장 중요하게 배울 점은 무엇인가요?

- Go to your mom when you feel sick.
- Follow the doctor's advice.
- V Wash your hands to stay healthy.

p.35 Listen Again

스토리를 다시 들으며 빈칸에 알맞은 단어를 써 넣으세요.

Leo loves playing outside. He runs around the yard and digs in the dirt.
At lunch, Mom says, "Wash your hands!"
But Leo skips washing. "I'll do it later," he says.

Leo eats with his dirty hands. Germs get on his sandwich and glass.
That afternoon, Leo's nose starts running.
His throat hurts. "Why do I feel sick?"
Leo wonders.

Mom takes Leo to the doctor. The doctor says, "Germs can make you sick. Please follow these healthy habits."

At home, Leo washes his hands with soap.
"This is easy!" he says. Now, Leo follows the doctor's advice every day!

wash / outside / sick / nose / germ / doctor / dirt / soap / healthy / follow

p.36 Sentence Patterns

다음 필수 문형을 다양한 예문에 적용해 보세요.

1 He loves ___-ing.

- He loves playing outside.
- He loves riding his bike.
- He loves eating ice cream.

2 Mom takes ___ to ___.

- Mom takes Leo to the doctor.
- Mom takes me to the park.
- Mom takes my brother to the dentist.

Word Box: • eat ice cream • ride his bike • sleepy • my brother, the dentist • me, the park • tired

p.37

3 They can make you ___.

- They can make you sick.
- They can make you tired.
- They can make you sleepy.

Try Writing

1. 그는 장난감 고치는 것을 매우 좋아해요. (fix toys) — He loves fixing toys.
2. 엄마는 우리를 도서관에 데려가요. (us, the library) — Mom takes us to the library.
3. 그것들은 너를 슬프게 만들 수 있어. (sad) — They can make you sad.

p.38 Think More

Healthy Habits

- Wash your hands often.
- Wear a mask on dusty days.
- Drink plenty of water.
- Eat healthy food.
- Get enough rest.
- Cover your mouth when you cough.

water mask healthy hands rest

건강 습관

- 손을 자주 씻어요.
- 먼지가 많은 날에는 마스크를 써요.
- 물을 많이 마셔요.
- 건강한 음식을 먹어요.
- 충분히 쉬어요.
- 기침할 때 입을 가려요.

Unit 3

Hello! We Are Signs

안녕! 우리는 표지판이에요

Key Words

sign 표지판	**museum** 박물관	**touch** 만지다	**break** 깨지다, 부서지다
dangerous 위험한	**bring** 가져오다	**photo** 사진	**flash** 반짝임

Sentence Patterns

• **Don't touch** ______ **.**	~을 만지지 마세요.
• **Remember to** ______ **.**	~하는 것을 기억하세요.
• **Thank you for** ______ **-ing .**	~해줘서 감사합니다.

Story Reading

p.42

우리는 박물관에 있는 "하지 마세요" 표지판들이에요.
우리는 중요한 메시지를 가지고 있어요.
우리에 대해 알고 싶나요?

p.43

나는 "손대지 마세요." 표지판이에요.
나는 이렇게 말해요. "박물관에 있는 물건들을 만지지 마세요."
어떤 것들은 쉽게 깨질 수 있어요.

나는 "뛰지 마세요." 표지판이에요.
나는 이렇게 말해요. "걸으세요, 뛰지 마세요."
박물관 안에서 뛰는 것은 위험할 수 있어요.

p.44

나는 "음식 금지" 표지판이에요.
나는 이렇게 말해요. "음식을 가져오거나 안에서 먹지 마세요."
음식은 지저분하게 만들 수 있어요.

나를 봐요, "사진 금지" 표지판이에요.
나는 이렇게 말해요. "사진을 찍지 마세요."
(카메라) 플래시는 미술품을 손상시킬 수 있어요.

p.45

우리는 박물관을 안전하게 지키는 데 도움이 돼요.
규칙을 따르는 것을 기억하세요.
우리의 말을 들어줘서 고마워요.

Answers

p.41

A 단어와 우리말 뜻을 알맞게 연결하세요.

1 bring — 가져오다
2 flash — 번쩍임
3 dangerous — 위험한
4 sign — 표지판

B 다음 우리말 뜻에 맞는 단어를 찾아 동그라미 하고 한 번 쓰세요.

p	h	o	t	o	y	r	h
w	k	s	j	f	a	d	e
l	u	b	n	v	e	k	p
c	f	r	t	o	u	c	h
m	q	e	g	l	f	s	b
b	i	a	t	j	c	z	i
s	n	k	q	v	y	o	n
m	u	s	e	u	m	p	w

1 박물관 museum
2 만지다 touch
3 사진 photo
4 깨지다, 부서지다 break

p.46 Comprehension

A 보기에서 알맞은 단어를 골라 빈칸에 쓰세요.

sign dangerous flash museum touch

1 We are some "do not" sign s in museums.
2 Flash can damage art.
3 I say, "Don't touch the things in the museum."
4 We help keep museum s safe.
5 Running inside can be dangerous

p.47

B 들려주는 문장을 올바른 순서로 쓴 다음, 알맞은 그림에 번호를 쓰세요.

1 some things / easily. / can break → Some things can break easily.
2 a mess. / food / can make → Food can make a mess.
3 inside. / don't bring / or eat food → Don't bring or eat food inside.

3 2 1

C 다음 문장이 옳으면 T(True), 틀리면 F(False)에 동그라미 하세요.

1 The "No running" sign tells you to walk inside. — T
2 The "No photos" sign tells you not to bring food. — F
3 The signs keep museums messy. — F

p.48

D 그림에 맞는 문장이 되도록 빈칸에 알맞은 단어를 찾아 쓰세요.

I say, "Don't touch the things in the museum."
I say, "Walk, don't run ."
I say, "Don't take photo s."
I say, "Don't bring or eat food inside."

photo run touch bring

Think & Say

주변에서 흔히 볼 수 있는 안내 표지판이에요. 각각 무엇을 의미할까요?

ⓓ ⓑ ⓐ ⓒ

ⓐ Bicycle Lane (자전거 도로)
ⓑ Caution (주의)
ⓒ Exit (출구)
ⓓ Restroom (화장실)

p.49 Listen Again

스토리를 다시 들으며 빈칸에 알맞은 단어를 써 넣으세요.

We are some "do not" sign s in museums. We have important messages. Do you want to learn about us?

I am the "No touching" sign. I say, "Don't touch the things in the museum." Some things can break easily.

I am the "No running" sign. I say, "Walk, don't run ." Running inside can be dangerous

I am the "No food" sign. I say, "Don't bring or eat food inside." Food can make a mess . Look at me, the "No photo s" sign. I say, "Don't take photos." Flash can damage art.

We help keep museum safe. Remember to follow the rules. Thank you for listening to us.

run damage touch break museum sign bring mess photo dangerous

p.50 Sentence Patterns

다음 필수 문형을 다양한 예문에 적용해 보세요.

1 Don't touch ____. ~을 만지지 마세요.

미술품을 만지지 마세요. Don't touch the art .
뜨거운 물을 만지지 마세요. Don't touch the hot water
칼을 만지지 마세요. Don't touch the knife .

2 Remember to ____. ~하는 것을 기억하세요.

규칙을 지키는 것을 기억하세요. Remember to follow the rules .
네 숙제를 하는 것을 기억하세요. Remember to do your homework
네 책을 가져오는 것을 기억하세요. Remember to bring your book

Word Box: bring your book 네 책을 가져오다 · share 나누다 · the knife 칼 · do your homework 네 숙제를 하다 · come 오다 · the hot water 뜨거운 물

p.51

3 Thank you for ____-ing. ~해줘서 고맙습니다.

들어줘서 감사합니다. Thank you for listening .
와줘서 감사합니다. Thank you for coming .
나눠줘서 감사합니다. Thank you for sharing .

Try Writing 배운 필수 문형을 활용해 영작해 보세요.

1 네 점심을 먹는 것을 기억하세요. (eat your lunch) Remember to eat your lunch.
2 벌레를 만지지 마세요. (the bug) Don't touch the bug.
3 도와줘서 감사합니다. (help) Thank you for helping.

p.52 Think More

Museum Signs

박물관에서는 어떤 규칙을 지켜야 할까요? 다음 상황에 알맞은 말을 완성하세요.

This is so nice! — Please don't touch .
I'm hungry. — Sorry, you can't eat .
Follow me! — Please don't run .
Can I take a photo? — Please don't take photos here.

eat run photos touch

박물관 표지판들

"이거 정말 멋지다!"
– 만지지 마세요.

"나는 배고파."
– 미안하지만 먹을 수 없어요.

"날 따라와!"
– 뛰지 마세요.

"사진 찍어도 돼요?"
– 여기에서 사진을 찍지 마세요.

Unit 4

The Rainbow Garden

무지개 정원

Key Words

paint (물감 등을) 칠하다, 물감	**garden** 정원	**dip** 살짝 담그다	**stamp** (도장 등을) 찍다
handprint 손바닥 자국	**rub** 문지르다	**purple** 보라색의, 보라색	**rainbow** 무지개

Sentence Patterns

• **She paints ______ ______.**	그녀는 ~을 …으로 칠해요.
• **It turns ______.**	그것이 ~으로 변해요.
• **Look at ______!**	~을 봐요!

Story Reading

p.56

미아는 그림을 그리고 있어요.
그녀는 노란색을 매우 좋아해요.
그녀는 큰 종이를 노란색으로 칠해요.
"아름다운 노란색 정원이 될 거야." 그녀가 말해요.

p.57

미아의 여동생 루나가 들어와요.
루나는 빨간 물감에 손을 담가요.
그녀는 노란 그림에 손바닥을 찍어요.
와! 손자국이 주황색으로 변해요!

p.58

루나는 다른 손을 사용해요.
그 손을 파란 물감에 담가요.
다시 그림에 손자국을 찍어요.
이번에는 초록색으로 변해요!

미아는 좋은 생각이 떠올라요.
그녀는 루나의 두 손을 서로 문질러요.

이제 물감이 보라색으로 변해요!

p.59

"루나, 여기에 손자국을 찍어 봐!" 미아가 말해요.
곧 그림이 완성돼요.
아름다운 무지개 정원을 보세요!
둘은 함께 미소 짓고 웃어요.

Answers

p.55

A

1. rainbow
2. rub
3. paint
4. handprint

B

t, a, g, r, d, i, p, u, r, l, n

p.60 Comprehension

A

rainbow rub stamp dip purple

1. Luna dip s her hand in red paint.
2. Look at the beautiful rainbow garden!
3. Now, the paint turns purple !
4. Mia rub s both of Luna's hands together.
5. Luna stamp s the picture again.

p.61

B

1. a beautiful / yellow garden. / it will be
→ It will be a beautiful yellow garden.
2. yellow. / her big paper / she paints
→ She paints her big paper yellow.
3. orange! / the handprint / turns
→ The handprint turns orange!

3 1 2

C

1. This story is about painting a colorful garden. (T)
2. Mia paints her paper yellow. (T)
3. Blue and yellow make green. (T)

p.62

D

Actions	Colors
Mia paints her paper yellow.	1st circle
Luna stamps red paint on the yellow picture.	2nd circle
Luna stamps blue paint on the yellow picture.	3rd circle
Mia rubs Luna's hands together. (red + blue)	4th circle

Think & Say

blue / green / red / yellow / purple

I like ______ because ______

나는 ______을 좋아해. 왜냐하면 ______ 때문이야.

p.63 Listen Again

Mia is painting a picture. She loves yellow. She paint s her big paper yellow. "It will be a beautiful yellow garden." she says.

Her little sister, Luna, comes in. Luna dip s her hand in red paint. She stamp s it on the yellow picture. Wow! The handprint turns orange!

Luna uses her other hand. She dips it in blue paint. She stamps the picture again. This time, it turns green !
Mia gets an idea. She rub s both of Luna's hands together. Now, the paint turns purple !

"Luna, stamp your hands here!" Mia says. Soon, the picture is done. Look at the beautiful rainbow garden! They smile and laugh together.

blue, purple, rainbow, rub, green, handprint, stamp, garden, paint, dip

p.64 Sentence Patterns

1 She paints ______ ______.

She paints her big paper yellow .

She paints the wall blue .

She paints the door green .

2 It turns ______.

It turns green .

It turns orange .

It turns purple .

Word Box: the house, orange, the wall, blue, the sky, purple, the door, green

p.65

3 Look at ______ !

Look at the garden !

Look at the house !

Look at the sky !

Try Writing

1. (the house, red) She paints the house red.
2. (blue) It turns blue.
3. (the rainbow) Look at the rainbow!

p.66 Think More

Mixing Colors

Mix red and yellow to make orange .

Mix yellow and blue to make green.

Mix red and blue to make purple .

Mix red and white to make pink .

색깔 섞기

- 빨강과 노랑을 섞어서 주황을 만드세요.
- 노랑과 파랑을 섞어서 초록을 만드세요.
- 빨강과 파랑을 섞어서 보라를 만드세요.
- 빨강과 하양을 섞어서 분홍을 만드세요.

Unit 5

Spooky Halloween Toast

으스스한 핼러윈 토스트

Key Words

toast 토스트	**spread** (버터 등을) 바르다	**add** 넣다, 추가하다	**mouth** 입
ghost 유령, 귀신	**raisin** 건포도	**bandage** 붕대	**spooky** 으스스한

Sentence Patterns

• **Let's make** ______ **!**	~을 만들자!
• **We're going to** ______ **.**	우리는 ~할 거예요.
• **It looks like** ______ **.**	그것은 ~처럼 보여요.

Story Reading

p.74

핼러윈 토스트를 만들자!
우리는 재미있는 괴물 얼굴을 만들 거예요.
이 토스트들은 만들기 쉽고 재미있어요.
준비됐나요?

p.75

아보카도 괴물 토스트

먼저, 토스트 한 조각에 아보카도를 펴 바르세요.
다음으로, 눈을 만들기 위해 올리브를 올리세요.
마지막으로, 입 모양에는 피망을 사용하세요.

바나나 유령 토스트

먼저, 토스트 한 조각에 땅콩버터를 바르세요.
다음으로, 바나나를 반으로 자르세요.
반쪽들을 토스트에 놓으세요.
그다음, 눈을 만들기 위해 건포도를 올리세요.

p.76

흰 유령 토스트

먼저, 토스트 한 조각에 크림치즈를 바르세요.
다음으로, 올리브로 재미있는 얼굴을 만들어 보세요.
이제 유령처럼 보여요!

미라 토스트

먼저, 토스트 한 조각에 햄을 놓으세요.
다음으로, 치즈 조각을 붕대처럼 올리세요.
그다음, 올리브로 마무리하세요.

p.77

모든 으스스한 토스트가 준비됐어요!
가족과 친구들과 함께 토스트를 나누어 먹어요.
오싹한 핼러윈을 보내세요!

Answers

p.73

A 단어와 우리말 뜻을 알맞게 연결하세요.

1. mouth — 입
2. ghost — 유령, 귀신
3. add — 넣다, 추가하다
4. spooky — 으스스한

B 다음 우리말 뜻에 맞는 단어를 찾아 동그라미 하고 한 번 쓰세요.

r	a	i	s	i	n	b	t
d	u	j	o	g	e	n	o
m	h	c	q	k	s	j	a
i	r	y	l	t	p	u	s
t	x	h	v	z	r	d	t
p	j	s	e	y	e	m	f
y	b	a	n	d	a	g	e
f	w	l	r	k	d	i	c

1. 붕대 — bandage
2. (버터 등을) 바르다 — spread
3. 건포도 — raisin
4. 토스트 — toast

Unit 5 73

p.78 3 확장 Comprehension

A 보기에서 알맞은 단어를 골라 빈칸에 쓰세요.

place ghost spread toast mouth

1. First, place ham on a slice of toast.
2. All the spooky toast is ready!
3. Now it looks like a ghost !
4. Finally, use bell pepper for the mouth .
5. First, spread cream cheese on a slice of toast.

78

p.79

B 들려주는 문장을 올바른 순서로 쓴 다음, 알맞은 그림에 번호를 쓰세요.

1. like bandages. / add / cheese strips
→ Add cheese strips like bandages.
2. spread / on a slice of toast. / peanut butter
→ Spread peanut butter on a slice of toast.
3. raisins / for the eyes. / add
→ Add raisins for the eyes.

3 2 1

C 다음 문장이 옳으면 T(True), 틀리면 F(False)에 동그라미 하세요.

1. This story is about making Halloween toast. (T)
2. Use ham for the monster's mouth. (F)
3. Add cheese strips for the mummy's bandages. (T)

Unit 5 79

p.80

D 설명을 잘 읽고 알맞은 토스트 이름을 빈칸에 쓰세요.

Avocado Monster Toast　Banana Ghost Toast　White Ghost Toast　Mummy Toast

- Add cheese strips like bandages, and finish it with olives. — Mummy Toast
- Spread avocado on a slice of toast, and add olives for the eyes. — Avocado Monster Toast
- Spread cream cheese on a slice of toast, and make a fun face with olives. — White Ghost Toast

Think & Say

어떤 토스트를 만들고 싶나요? 토스트에 넣을 재료를 골라 보세요.

□ banana □ raisins
□ avocado □ olives
□ mango □ cream cheese
□ cheese □

My spooky toast will be delicious because it has ______.

내 으스스한 토스트는 ______가 있어서 맛있을 거야.

80

p.81 Listen Again

● 스토리를 다시 들으며 빈칸에 알맞은 단어를 써 넣으세요.

Let's make Halloween toast ! We're going to make fun monster faces. These are easy and fun to make. Are you ready?

[Avocado Monster Toast] First, spread avocado on a slice of toast. Next, add olives for the eyes. Finally, use bell pepper for the mouth .

[Banana Ghost Toast] First, spread peanut butter on a slice of toast. Next, cut a banana in half. Put the halves on the toast. Then, add raisin s for the eyes.

[White Ghost Toast] First, spread cream cheese on a slice of toast. Next, make a fun face with olives. Now it looks like a ghost !

[Mummy Toast] First, place ham on a slice of toast. Next, add cheese strips like bandage s. Then, finish it with olives.

All the spooky toast is ready! Share the toast with your family and friends. Have a spooky Halloween!

face add spooky raisin mouth ghost spread toast share bandage

Unit 5 81

p.82 3 확장 Sentence Patterns

● 다음 필수 문형을 다양한 예문에 적용해 보세요.

1 Let's make ______ ! ~을 만들자!

- 핼러윈 토스트를 만들자! Let's make Halloween toast !
- 샌드위치를 만들자! Let's make a sandwich !
- 피자를 만들자! Let's make a pizza !

2 We're going to ______ . 우리는 ~할 거예요.

- 우리는 재미있는 괴물 얼굴을 만들 거예요. We're going to make fun monster faces .
- 우리는 컴퓨터를 사용할 거예요. We're going to use the computer .
- 우리는 달걀을 살 거예요. We're going to buy some eggs .

Word Box: • a dragon 용 • buy some eggs 달걀을 사다 • a pizza 피자 • a sandwich 샌드위치 • use the computer 컴퓨터를 사용하다 • a cat 고양이

82

p.83

3 It looks like ______ . 그것은 ~처럼 보여요.

- 그것은 유령처럼 보여요. It looks like a ghost .
- 그것은 고양이처럼 보여요. It looks like a cat .
- 그것은 용처럼 보여요. It looks like a dragon .

Try Writing 배운 필수 문형을 활용해 영작해 보세요.

1. 쿠키를 만들자! (cookies) — Let's make cookies!
2. 그것은 호박처럼 보여요. (a pumpkin) — It looks like a pumpkin.
3. 우리는 피아노를 연주할 거예요. (play the piano) — We're going to play the piano.

Unit 5 83

p.84 Think More

Let's Make Spooky Toast!

★ 요리 재료가 적힌 메모를 보고 완성된 토스트를 찾아 연결하세요.

- □ mashed avocado □ sliced bell pepper □ sliced olives
- □ blueberries □ raspberries □ sliced cucumber
- □ peanut butter □ sliced banana □ some raisins
- □ eggs □ sliced cucumber □ sliced ham

* mashed 으깬 blueberry 블루베리 raspberry 산딸기 cucumber 오이

84

으스스한 토스트를 만들자!

Unit 6

A Trip to Grandma's House

할머니 댁으로 가는 여행

Key Words

map 지도	**fence** 울타리	**park** 공원	**right** 오른쪽으로, 오른쪽의
corner 모퉁이	**across** 건너서	**wave** (손을) 흔들다	**afraid** 두려워하는

Sentence Patterns

• **There is** ______ **on the corner.**	모퉁이에 ~이 있어요.
• **I see** ______ ______**-ing .**	나는 ~가 …하는 것을 봐요.
• **I was afraid to** ______ **.**	나는 ~하는 것이 무서웠어요.

Story Reading

p.88

나는 혼자서 할머니 댁에 갈 거예요.
이 지도는 내가 길을 찾는 데 도움을 줄 거예요.
나는 여기 살아요, 빨간 울타리가 있는 집 옆이에요.
할머니 댁은 큰 공원 근처에 있어요.

p.89

먼저, 나는 오크 거리를 따라 걸어요.
그다음, 메인 거리로 오른쪽으로 돌아요.
보세요! 모퉁이에 빵집이 있어요.
나는 왼쪽으로 돌아 도서관 쪽으로 걸어가요.

p.90

할머니 댁은 길 건너편에 있어요.
그 옆에는 큰 나무가 있어요.
할머니 댁에는 초록색 문이 있어요.
창문에서 할머니가 손을 흔드는 게 보여요.

p.91

처음에는 혼자 가는 것이 무서웠어요.
하지만 이 지도가 내게 정말 도움이 되었어요.
할머니 댁에 또 가고 싶어 너무 기대돼요!

Answers

p.87

A 단어와 우리말 뜻을 알맞게 연결하세요.

1 across — 건너서
2 right — 오른쪽으로, 오른쪽의
3 fence — 울타리
4 wave — (손을) 흔들다

B 우리말 뜻에 맞는 단어가 되도록 빈칸에 알맞은 글자를 쓰세요.

① 지도 — map
② 공원 — park
③ 모퉁이 — corner
④ 두려워하는 — afraid

m, c, o, p a r k, n, e, a f r a i d

p.92 Comprehension

A 보기에서 알맞은 단어를 골라 빈칸에 쓰세요.

across map corner park fence

1 I live here, next to the house with a red fence.
2 Grandma's house is across the street.
3 This map will help me find the way.
4 There is a bakery on the corner.
5 Grandma's house is near the big park.

p.93

B 들려주는 문장을 올바른 순서로 쓴 다음, 알맞은 그림에 번호를 쓰세요.

1 afraid / I was / to go alone.
→ I was afraid to go alone.
2 next to / there is a big tree / Grandma's house.
→ There is a big tree next to Grandma's house.
3 Grandma waving / from her window. / I see
→ I see Grandma waving from her window.

1 3 2

C 다음 문장이 옳으면 T(True), 틀리면 F(False)에 동그라미 하세요.

1 She uses a map to go to Grandma's house. — T
2 Grandma's house is near the big park. — T
3 Grandma's house has a red door. — F

p.94

D 지도를 보고, 할머니 집에 가는 방법을 순서대로 적으세요.

1 ⓑ → 2 ⓐ → 3 ⓒ → 4 ⓓ

ⓐ Turn right onto Main Street.
ⓑ Walk along Oak Street.
ⓒ Turn left and walk toward the library.
ⓓ Grandma's house is across the street.

Think & Say

혼자서 해 보고 싶은 일을 골라 문장을 완성해 보세요.

- take the bus
- walk my dog
- buy a snack at a store
- visit my friend

I want to ______ by myself.

나는 혼자서 ______ 하고 싶어.

p.95 Listen Again

스토리를 다시 들으며 빈칸에 알맞은 단어를 써 넣으세요.

I'm going to Grandma's house on my own. This map will help me find the way. I live here, next to the house with a red fence. Grandma's house is near the big park.

First, I walk along Oak Street. Then, I turn right onto Main Street. Look! There is a bakery on the corner. I turn left and walk toward the library.

Grandma's house is across the street. There is a big tree next to it. Her house has a green door. I see Grandma waving from her window.

At first, I was afraid to go alone. But this map really helped me. I can't wait to visit Grandma again!

right, next, park, fence, library, map, corner, across, afraid, window

p.96 Sentence Patterns

다음 필수 문형을 다양한 예문에 적용해 보세요.

1 There is ______ on the corner.

There is a bakery on the corner.
There is a bus stop on the corner.
There is a flower shop on the corner.

2 I see ______ -ing.

I see Grandma waving.
I see a cat sleeping.
I see a dog barking.

Word Box: a flower shop, hold the frog, a cat, sleep, a bus stop, a dog, bark, climb the ladder

p.97

3 I was afraid to ______.

I was afraid to go alone.
I was afraid to hold the frog.
I was afraid to climb the ladder.

Try Writing

1 모퉁이에 벤치가 하나 있어요. (a bench)
There is a bench on the corner.
2 나는 엄마가 운전하는 것을 봐요. (Mom, drive)
I see Mom driving.
3 나는 거미를 만지는 것이 무서웠어요. (touch the spider)
I was afraid to touch the spider.

p.98 Think More

Reading a Map

First, walk along Oak Street.
Then, turn left onto Main Street.
There are maple trees on the corner.
Turn right onto Maple Street.
Keep walking toward the church.
Across from the church, and you'll find the library.

지도 읽기

먼저, 오크 거리를 따라 걸으세요.
그다음, 메인 거리로 왼쪽으로 도세요.
모퉁이에 단풍나무들이 있어요.
메이플 거리로 오른쪽으로 도세요.
교회 쪽으로 계속 걸으세요.
교회 맞은편에 도서관이 보일 거예요.

Unit 7

Tim Learns the Rules

팀이 규칙을 배워요

Key Words

rule 규칙	**cafeteria** (학교) 식당	**hallway** 복도	**shout** 소리치다
bump into 부딪히다	**pile** 쌓다	**mess** 엉망인 상태	**stomachache** 복통

Sentence Patterns

- **Never** ______. — 절대 ~하지 말아요.
- **He has** ______. — 그는 ~가 있어요.
- **This is why we** ______. — 이것이 우리가 ~하는 이유예요.

Story Reading

p.102

우리는 점심시간 종소리를 들어요.
선생님이 말해요, "수업이 끝났어요. 점심시간이에요. 기억하세요, 절대 뛰거나 다른 사람들을 밀지 마세요. 이 규칙들은 우리가 즐겁게 점심을 먹도록 도와줘요."

p.103

우리는 식당으로 걸어가요.
하지만 팀은 복도를 달려가요.
"너무 배고파!" 팀이 외쳐요.
팀은 친구들과 부딪혀요.

p.104

우리는 줄을 서서 음식을 기다려요.
우리는 먹을 수 있을 만큼만 가져가요.

하지만 팀은 줄을 건너뛰고 맨 첫 번째로 가요.
그는 음식을 너무 많이 쌓아 올려요.

p.105

팀은 너무 많이, 너무 빨리 먹어요.
그의 음식이 (주변을) 엉망으로 만들어요.

교실에 돌아와서, 팀은 배가 아파요.
선생님이 말해요. "팀, 이래서 우리가 규칙을 지키는 거란다."

Answers

p.101

A 단어와 우리말 뜻을 알맞게 연결하세요.

1 pile — 쌓다
2 cafeteria — (학교) 식당
3 bump into — 부딪히다
4 stomachache — 복통

B 다음 우리말 뜻에 맞는 단어를 찾아 동그라미 하고 한 번 쓰세요.

h	d	o	m	r	i	a	s
a	j	b	z	f	u	p	h
l	t	r	y	v	i	k	o
l	a	q	m	e	s	s	u
w	e	f	w	c	t	d	t
a	p	r	u	l	e	x	g
y	h	y	k	w	j	u	o
q	c	g	s	r	n	x	b

1 소리치다 shout
2 복도 hallway
3 규칙 rule
4 엉망인 상태 mess

p.106 Comprehension

A 보기에서 알맞은 단어를 골라 빈칸에 쓰세요.

wait bump rule hallway stomachache

1 These **rule**s help us enjoy lunch.
2 We **wait** in line for our food.
3 Back in class, Tim has a **stomachache**.
4 Tim runs down the **hallway**.
5 Tim **bump**s into his friends.

p.107

B 들려주는 문장을 올바른 순서로 쓴 다음, 알맞은 그림에 번호를 쓰세요.

1 wait in line / for our food. / we → **We wait in line for our food.**
2 piles on / he / too much food. → **He piles on too much food.**
3 he / the hallway. / runs down → **He runs down the hallway.**

2 1 3

C 다음 문장이 옳으면 T(True), 틀리면 F(False)에 동그라미 하세요.

1 Tim walks slowly to the cafeteria. **F**
2 Tim skips the line. **T**
3 Tim gets a headache. **F**

p.108

D 다음을 읽고 올바른 행동은 'Dos' 칸에, 나쁜 행동은 'Don'ts' 칸에 기호를 쓰세요.

Dos(좋은 행동)	Don'ts(나쁜 행동)
Wait in line.	Skip the line.
Follow the rules.	Push others.
ⓐ	ⓑ
ⓔ	ⓒ
ⓕ	ⓓ

ⓐ Walk to the cafeteria. ⓑ Make a mess. ⓒ Bump into others. ⓓ Pile on too much food. ⓔ Take only as much as you can eat. ⓕ Walk down the hallway.

Think & Say

이 글에 가장 알맞은 교훈에 ✓ 표시하세요.

✓ Following the rules helps us enjoy lunch.
☐ Eating healthy food keeps us strong.
☐ Sharing food with friends makes us happy.

p.109 Listen Again

스토리를 다시 들으며 빈칸에 알맞은 단어를 써 넣으세요.

We hear the lunch bell. The teacher says, "Class is over. It's lunchtime. Remember, never run or **push** others. These **rule**s help us enjoy lunch."

We walk to the **cafeteria**. But Tim runs down the **hallway**. "I'm so hungry!" Tim **shout**s. Tim **bump**s into his friends.

We **wait** in line for our food. We only take as much as we can eat. But Tim skips the line and goes first. He **pile**s on too much food.

Tim eats too much, too fast. His food makes a big **mess**. Back in class, Tim has a **stomachache**. The teacher says, "Tim, this is why we follow the rules."

shout pile wait push hallway rule bump mess cafeteria stomachache

p.110 Sentence Patterns

다음 필수 문형을 다양한 예문에 적용해 보세요.

1 Never ___.

Never **run or push others**.
Never **play with fire**.
Never **waste food**.

2 He has ___.

He has **a stomachache**.
He has **a headache**.
He has **a fever**.

Word Box: waste food, a headache, wear a coat, play with fire, a fever, eat vegetables

p.111

3 This is why we ___.

This is why we **follow the rules**.
This is why we **eat vegetables**.
This is why we **wear a coat**.

Try Writing 배운 필수 문형을 활용해 영작해 보세요.

1 절대 다른 사람들을 때리지 말아요. (hit others) **Never hit others.**
2 그는 감기에 걸렸어요. (a cold) **He has a cold.**
3 이것이 우리가 양치하는 이유예요. (brush our teeth) **This is why we brush our teeth.**

p.112 Think More

School Cafeteria Rules

Wait in **line** for your food.
Wash your **hands** before eating.
Take only as much as you can **eat**.
Eat slowly and chew well.
Carry your **tray** carefully.

tray line eat hands

학교 식당 규칙

- 줄을 서서 음식을 기다려요.
- 먹기 전에 손을 씻어요.
- 먹을 수 있는 만큼만 가져가요.
- 천천히 먹고 꼭꼭 씹어요.
- 식판은 조심해서 들어요.

Unit 8

A New Friend for Our Family

우리 가족의 새 친구

Key Words

meeting 회의	quiet 조용한	clean 깨끗한	couch 긴 의자, 소파
change 바꾸다	turtle 거북	move 움직이다	welcome 환영하다

Sentence Patterns

• They like to ______.	그들은 ~하는 것을 좋아해요.
• I will ______.	나는 ~할 거예요.
• It's important to ______.	~하는 것이 중요해요.

Story Reading

p.116

우리는 가족 회의를 하고 있어요.
우리는 새 동물 친구를 키우고 싶어요.
하지만 모두 다른 동물을 원해요.

p.117

개는 장난기 많고 활력이 넘쳐요.
그들은 밖에서 노는 것을 좋아해요.
나는 매일 개를 산책시킬 거예요.

나는 고양이를 매우 좋아해요.
그들은 조용하고 깨끗해요.
그들은 소파에서 자는 것을 좋아해요.
그들은 정말 귀여워요.

walk: 기본 뜻은 '걷다'예요. 하지만 '산책시키다' 또는 '산책, 걷기'라는 뜻으로도 쓰여요.

p.118

물고기는 알록달록하고 예뻐요.
물을 깨끗하게 유지하는 것이 중요해요.
나는 자주 물을 갈아줄 수 있어요.

거북은 아주 차분해요.
그들은 천천히 움직여서 산책이 필요 없어요.
거북은 우리에게 좋은 선택이에요.

p.119

모든 동물은 특별해요.
우리는 좋은 동물을 맞이하고 싶어요.
새 동물 친구를 가족처럼 사랑할 거예요.

Answers

p.115

A 단어와 우리말 뜻을 알맞게 연결하세요.

1 welcome — 환영하다
2 turtle — 거북
3 meeting — 회의
4 quiet — 조용한

B 우리말 뜻에 맞는 단어가 되도록 빈칸에 알맞은 글자를 쓰세요.

1 움직이다 — move
2 긴 의자, 소파 — couch
3 깨끗한 — clean
4 바꾸다 — change

Unit 8 115

p.120 Comprehension

A 보기에서 알맞은 단어를 골라 빈칸에 쓰세요.

change meeting turtle quiet welcome

1 Turtles are a good choice for us.
2 We want to welcome a good animal.
3 We're having a family meeting.
4 Cats are quiet and clean.
5 I can change the water often.

120

p.121

B 들려주는 문장을 올바른 순서로 쓴 다음, 알맞은 그림에 번호를 쓰세요.

1 clean. / It's important / to keep their water
→ It's important to keep their water clean.
2 my dog / I'll walk / every day.
→ I'll walk my dog every day.
3 sleeping / on the couch. / they enjoy
→ They enjoy sleeping on the couch.

3 1 2

C 다음 문장이 옳으면 T(True), 틀리면 F(False)에 동그라미 하세요.

1 This story is about a family meeting to get a dog. T (F)
2 Dogs don't need walks. T (F)
3 Turtles are playful and full of energy. T (F)

Unit 8 121

p.122

D 아래 문장을 읽고 각 동물의 특징과 돌보는 방법에 맞는 기호를 쓰세요.

	What are they like? (특징)	How do you take care of them? (돌보는 법)
dog	ⓑ	Walk them every day.
cat	quiet, clean	ⓒ
fish	colorful, pretty	ⓓ
turtle	ⓐ	Keep their tank clean.

ⓐ calm, slow
ⓑ playful, full of energy
ⓒ Give them a cozy bed.
ⓓ Change the water often.

Think & Say

우리 가족이 반려동물을 키운다면 어떤 동물이 좋을까요? 하나를 골라 보세요.

dog / cat / fish / turtle / parrot

I want a/an ______ because ______.

나는 ______을 원해. 왜냐하면 ______ 때문이야.

122

p.123 Listen Again

스토리를 다시 들으며 빈칸에 알맞은 단어를 써 넣으세요.

We're having a family meeting. We want to get a new animal friend. But everyone wants a different animal.

Dogs are playful and full of energy. They like to play outside. I'll walk my dog every day. I love cats. They are quiet and clean. They enjoy sleeping on the couch. They are so cute.

Fish are colorful and pretty. It's important to keep their water clean. I can change the water often. Turtles are very calm. They move slowly, so they don't need walks. Turtles are a good choice for us.

Every animal is special. We want to welcome a good animal. We'll love our new animal friend like family.

couch quiet special walk clean turtle welcome change meeting different

Unit 8 123

p.124 Sentence Patterns

다음 필수 문형을 다양한 예문에 적용해 보세요.

1 They like to ______. 그들은 ~하는 것을 좋아해요.

They like to play outside.
They like to jump on the bed.
They like to dance together.

2 I will ______. 나는 ~할 거예요.

I will walk my dog.
I will clean my room.
I will feed the fish.

Word Box
• jump on the bed • say thank you • dance together • feed the fish • clean my room • help others

124

p.125

3 It's important to ______. ~하는 것이 중요해요.

It's important to keep their water clean.
It's important to help others.
It's important to say thank you.

Try Writing 배운 필수 문형을 활용해 영작해 보세요.

1 나는 꽃에 물을 줄 거예요. (water the flowers)
I will water the flowers.
2 그들은 당근 먹는 것을 좋아해요. (eat carrots)
They like to eat carrots.
3 일찍 자는 것이 중요해요. (sleep early)
It's important to sleep early.

Unit 8 125

p.126 Think More

Taking Care of Pets

★ 반려동물을 키울 때 무엇이 필요할까요? 빈칸에 알맞은 단어를 찾아 쓰세요.

Pets need healthy food.
Pets need clean water to drink.
Pets need a quiet and safe place to rest.
Pets need to exercise every day.
Pets need love and kindness.

love rest food water

124

반려동물 돌보기

• 반려동물은 건강한 음식이 필요해요.
• 반려동물은 마실 수 있는 깨끗한 물이 필요해요.
• 반려동물은 조용하고 안전한 쉴 곳이 필요해요.
• 반려동물은 매일 운동이 필요해요.
• 반려동물은 사랑과 친절이 필요해요.

Review Test 정답

p.67

Review Test 1
(Unit ❶ – Unit ❹) / 25개

A 그림에 알맞은 단어를 고르세요.

1 ⓐ balloon **ⓑ umbrella** ⓒ present

2 ⓐ purple ⓑ flash **ⓒ handprint**

3 ⓐ wash ⓑ break **ⓒ touch**

4 ⓐ decorate **ⓑ stamp** ⓒ bring

5 **ⓐ invitation** ⓑ germ ⓒ garden

6 ⓐ sick **ⓑ healthy** ⓒ dangerous

Review Test 1 67

p.68

B 그림을 보고 알맞은 문장을 고르세요.

1 **ⓐ I make invitations for the party.**
ⓑ I give the invitations to my friends.

2 **ⓐ Mom brings him a sandwich.**
ⓑ Mom takes Leo to the doctor.

3 ⓐ "Don't touch the things in the museum."
ⓑ "Don't bring or eat food inside."

4 ⓐ Luna paints the paper blue.
ⓑ Luna stamps her hand on the picture.

C 알맞은 단어를 골라 문장을 완성하세요.

1 Leo washes his hands **ⓐ with** ⓑ on soap.

2 Mia is ⓐ paint **ⓑ painting** a picture.

3 Thank you for ⓐ listen **ⓑ listening** to us.

4 Oh no! It starts ⓐ rain **ⓑ to rain**.

68

p.69

D 짧은 글을 읽고 질문에 알맞은 대답을 고르세요.

1 다음 글에서 I가 가리키는 표지판을 고르세요.

I am a sign in the museum.
I say, "Walk, don't run."
Running inside can be dangerous.

ⓐ **ⓑ**

2 빈칸에 들어갈 알맞은 단어를 고르세요.

Luna dips her hand in blue paint.
She stamps it on the yellow picture.
It turns ________.

ⓐ green ⓑ orange

3 빈칸에 들어갈 알맞은 단어를 고르세요.

The doctor says, "Germs can make you ________. Please follow these healthy habits."

ⓐ sick ⓑ tall

4 빈칸에 들어갈 알맞은 문장을 고르세요.

My birthday is coming soon! I make invitations for the party. I give the invitations to my friends. ________________

ⓐ I can't wait for the vacation!
ⓑ I can't wait for the party!

Review Test 1 69

p.70

E 필수 패턴을 활용해 우리말에 알맞은 영어 문장을 완성하세요.

Don't touch ______.	He loves ______.
It starts to ______.	Look at ______!

1 그는 밖에서 노는 것을 매우 좋아해요.
→ He loves playing outside.

2 미술품을 만지지 마세요.
→ Don't touch the art.

3 비가 오기 시작해요.
→ It starts to rain.

4 저 정원을 봐요!
→ Look at the garden!

F 우리말에 알맞은 영어 문장을 쓰세요.

1 들어줘서 감사합니다. (for, you, thank, listening)
→ Thank you for listening.

2 이것은 최고의 생일이에요! (the best, this, is, ever, birthday)
→ This is the best birthday ever!

3 세균들이 너를 아프게 만들 수 있어. (can, germs, make, sick, you)
→ Germs can make you sick.

70

p.127

Review Test 2
(Unit ❺ – Unit ❽) / 25개

A 그림에 알맞은 단어를 고르세요.

1 ⓐ move ⓑ wave **ⓒ shout**

2 **ⓐ pile** ⓑ mess ⓒ slice

3 ⓐ couch **ⓑ fence** ⓒ map

4 ⓐ afraid **ⓑ quiet** ⓒ clean

5 ⓐ change ⓑ share **ⓒ spread**

6 **ⓐ across** ⓑ spooky ⓒ right

Review Test 2 127

p.128

B 그림을 보고 알맞은 문장을 고르세요.

1 **ⓐ Let's make Halloween toast!**
ⓑ All the spooky toast is ready!

2 ⓐ Tim piles on too much food.
ⓑ Tim bumps into his friends.

3 ⓐ The house has a red fence.
ⓑ The house has a green door.

4 **ⓐ We're having a family meeting.**
ⓑ We like to play outside.

C 알맞은 단어를 골라 문장을 완성하세요.

1 Grandma's house is **ⓐ near** ⓑ under the big park.

2 We're ⓐ go **ⓑ going** to make fun monster faces.

3 Cats **ⓐ enjoy** ⓑ enjoys sleeping on the couch.

4 Back in class, Tim **ⓐ has** ⓑ have a stomachache.

128

p.129

D 짧은 글을 읽고 질문에 알맞은 대답을 고르세요.

1 다음 설명을 참고해 알맞은 토스트를 고르세요.

First, spread cream cheese on a slice of toast. Next, make a fun face with olives. Now it looks like a ghost!

ⓐ **ⓑ**

2 다음 글을 읽고, They가 가리키는 대상을 고르세요.

They are very calm.
They move slowly.
They don't need walks.

ⓐ turtles ⓑ dogs

3 빈칸에 들어갈 알맞은 단어를 고르세요.

The teacher says, "It's lunchtime. Remember, never run or push others. These ________ help us enjoy lunch."

ⓐ games **ⓑ rules**

4 빈칸에 들어갈 알맞은 단어를 고르세요.

I'm going to Grandma's house on my own. This ________ will help me find the way.

ⓐ map ⓑ couch

Review Test 2 129

p.130

E 필수 패턴을 활용해 우리말에 알맞은 영어 문장을 완성하세요.

I was afraid to ______.	This is why we ______.
They like to ______.	We're going to ______.

1 우리는 달걀을 살 거예요.
→ We're going to buy some eggs.

2 이것이 우리가 채소를 먹는 이유예요.
→ This is why we eat vegetables.

3 그들은 함께 춤추는 것을 좋아해요.
→ They like to dance together.

4 나는 개구리를 잡는 것이 무서웠어요.
→ I was afraid to hold the frog.

F 우리말에 알맞은 영어 문장을 쓰세요.

1 다른 사람을 돕는 것이 중요해요. (help, it's, others, to, important)
→ It's important to help others.

2 나는 내 방을 청소할 거예요. (will, my room, clean, I)
→ I will clean my room.

3 나는 고양이 한 마리가 자고 있는 것을 봐요. (a cat, I, sleeping, see)
→ I see a cat sleeping.

130

"방법이 다르면 결과가 달라집니다"

리딩 실력을 껑충 키우는

기적만의 3-Step 완전학습

기적의 영어리딩

* 전문가가 설계한 6단계 리딩 프로그램으로 빈틈없는 영어 문해력 완성!

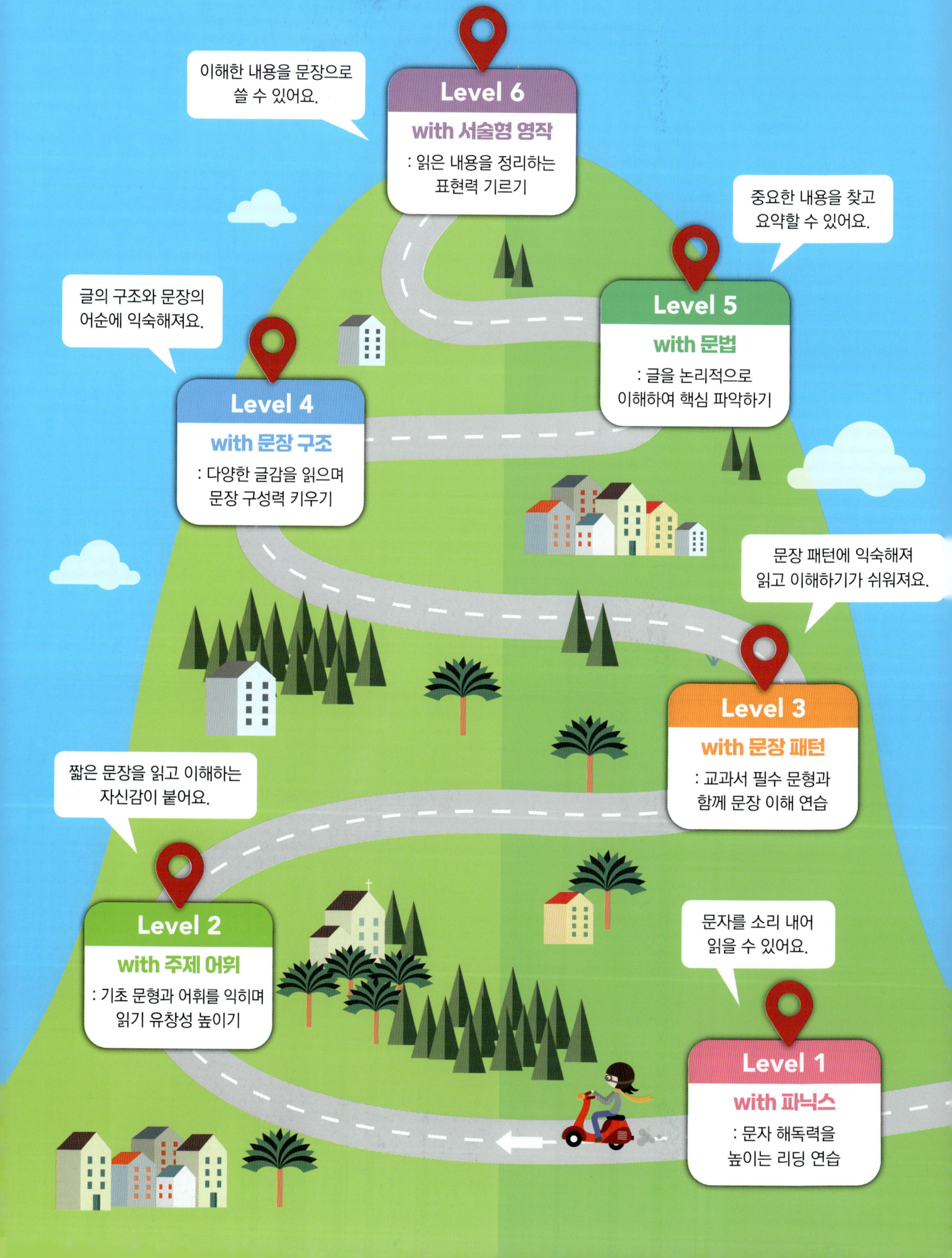